M000103594

The Nu Naybahood Funetic Ebonic Dictionary

BY D. MUNYUNGO JACKSON 1998

Published By
Milligan Books

Cover Design
Icehill UltraMedia

Illustrations By
Darryl "Wolf" Jackson, Jr.

Formatting By
AbarCo Business Services

Copyright © 1998 by D. Munyungo Jackson
Los Angeles, California
All rights reserved
Printed and Bound in the United States of America

Published and Distributed by:
Milligan Books
an imprint of Professional Business Consultants
1425 W. Manchester, Suite B,
Los Angeles, California 90047
(213) 750-3592

First Printing, October 1998
10 9 8 7 6 5 4 3 2 1

ISBN 1- 881524-39-6

All rights reserved. No part of this book may be reproduced in whole or in part, in any form or by any means, electronic or mechanical, including photocopying, recording or by any information storage and retrieval system, without permission in writing from the author. Address inquires to *Milligan Books,* 1425 W. Manchester, Suite B, Los Angeles, California 90047, (213) 750-3592

Printed in the United States of America

Preface

First of all, I love my people! (Some of us CAN be a little hard headed, and hard on each other, BUT-)

I love the fact that we have our own way of doing things, of expressing ourselves, and of communicating. We understand what each other is doing, saying, and feeling. Because of this special way of doing things, we have influenced the world with our language, our music, dance, and sports.

Unfortunately, most of us don't share in the rewards and benefits of that influence, and are sometimes the butt of jokes from people who really don't understand the nuances in our culture. For instance-

In late 1996, a group of educators in the San Francisco Bay area tried, unsuccessfully, to get funding to make Ebonics an official language in the public school system. The premise was that African American children had their own way of speaking and writing that was understood by them, and by most teachers, but was not con-sidered "proper english." News of the Ebonics proposal sparked many debates among African Americans, with most opposing it. It also sparked tons of jokes and stories over the Internet-some funny, most not-and most racists! Stories of how supposedly Black people talk. I know some of it was meant to be funny, but I didn't see it that way because it was not based on the truth. How could it be when the information didn't originate in the Black communities or environments!

Ebonics is not new. It goes back even before the time of slavery in the U.S. There are many respectable books written on the subject of Ebonics, Black english, and the history and evolution of language and of people of African descent. But not until the case of the "unsuccessful Ebonic funding" did the nation, and the world, pay any attention to the word "Ebonics" and the way us Black folks talk!

I do understand that most of the jokes on the Internet were fabricated for laughs. So I, and many others, began to listen more closely to how we DO speak, say things, come up with words that mean certain things, and use old words and change the meaning, without fabrication. And you know what? It's funny because it's real life!
In this book, I've collected words and terms that we use everyday. Some old, a lot new. Some of these words, when you read them, are going to be hard to figure out at first because they look funny. Some of these words are actually 2 or 3 words put together, but the way some of us speak, they sound like one word. For example: "WAOUNCHU" If you can't figure out how to say it, then it is important to read on because then

you'll find the word broken down phonetically into syllables, with the accent on the upper case letters. For example: (WA-oun-chu) Then it's used in a sentence, and then translated. Some of the words even come with an "alternative english" (*alt. eng.*) usage for you proper speaking folks!

After reading many of these words, terms, and sentences, I'm sure you'll say "Yep, I've said THAT before!" Or else you've heard someone else say it.

Now, the purpose of this book is mostly for entertainment, although there may be some educational value for those of you who are not familiar with some of the terms us Black Folks use. I say entertainment, because it is NOT to be mistaken for an addition, or a re-placement, for some of the great and serious work done on of Black English. Nor will you find most of these words in Webster's-or anybody else's-dictionary! Cept this one, which I call "THE NU NABAHOOD FUNETIC EBONIC DICTIONARY."

KEY

(term)- **in parentheses**- The word broken down phonetically into syllables, with the accent on the upper case (capital) letters.

ebncs.- **ebonics**- How the term is used in a sentence.

translation- **translation**- What the term means, or its definition, and correct spelling.

alt.eng.- **alternative english**- (In other words) another way of using the term without using the exact words. A more "proper" way, if you will.

ansr.- **answer**- Some of the words are used in a question / answer situation.

Ah got a buncha old **ABLUMS** by Coo-lina Gang, Sly, The Parlaments, and James Brown!

A

AAHKIN (AAH-kin) *ebncs.*- Dounbe *aahkin*
like u-ono whadum taunmot!
translation- Acting... Don't be ACTING like
you don't know what I'm talking about!
(*also see* **AAKTIN)**

AAKAHALL (AAK-ka-hall) You godda get some
aakahall and rub it on that bump on yo
head.
translation- Alcohol (the rubbing kind)

AAKAHALLIC (AAK-ka-HALL-lick) Dat boy
drink too much, I think he's an *aakahallic.*
translation- Alcoholic

AAKLAK (AAK-lack) **Aaklak** ya got some sense!
or- If you don't know, *aaklak* you know!
translation- Act like...

AAKS (AXE) If you don't know, waounchu *aaks*
somebody.
translation- Ask (asssk!)

AAKTIN (AAK-tin) I heard you was *aaktin* up
  in school today.
  or- You just *aaktin* like that cause your
  friends are here.
  translation- Acting (*also see* AAHKIN)

ABLE-DUH (A-buh-duh) Ahbe *able-duh* call you
  next week when my phone gets cut back on.
  translation- Able to...

ABLUM (AAH-blum) Ah got a buncha old
  ablums by Coo-lina Gang, Sly, The
  Parlaments, and James Brown!
  translation- Album (You know, records...
  vinyl...)

ABOUCHO (ah-BOUT-cho) Yo man, *aboutcho*
  breathe!
  alt. eng.- Excuse me, can we talk ABOUT
  YOUR need for some mints, or a colon
  cleanse? (*also see* BOUTCHO)

ACHA (AT-cha) Ah git back *acha* roun seb'n.
  translation- At ya...

ACHU (aah-CHU) **1.** Whachu lookin at? (*ansr.*)
  I'm lookin *achu*.
  2. *ACHU!* (*response*) God bless you!
  translation- **1.** At you... **2.** Get a Kleenex.

AFTA (AF-ta) Am *afta* you! *or-* And *afta* you finish moppin, go inare and do dem dishes! *translation-* After

AH-AINE (AH-aine) *Ah-aine* got no money! *or-* Ya'll can go and get high if ya'll want, but *ah-aine* widdit! (*also see* WIDDIT) *translation-* I ain't... I don't... I won't... I'm not... I will not...

AHAINEVA (AH-ain-NEH-va) *Ahaineva* goin back to that place again! *translation-* I ain't never... *or-* I will not, ever again...

AHAINMAD-ATCHA (AH-AINE-mad-at-cha) *Ahainmad*-atcha! *translation-* I'm not mad at you... I'm not disagreeing with you... We still good...

AHBE (AH-bee) Well, *ahbe* damn! *or- Ahbe* back inna minuet. *translation-* I'll be...

AHBEDARE (ah-b-dare) Don't worry, *ahbedare* round six. *translation-* I'll be there...

AHDABIN (AH-DA-bin) If it was me, *ahdabin* all over dat hoe!
translation- I'd have been... *or-* I would have been ...
alt. eng.- If it were up to me, I WOULD HAVE BEEN there to show her a great time.

AHDONE (AH-done) *Ahdone* already tolju, you mess wit that stuff, you go-da jail!
translation / alt. eng.- I HAVE already informed you of the consequences of your involvement in the abuse of such illicit substances.

AH-GODDA (AH-GA-da) **1.** *Ah-godda* get me a job! **2.** *Ah-godda* bigo corn on my little toe on my leff foot!
translation- **1.** I've Got To... **2.** I've Got A...

AH-GODIT (AH-ga-dit) *Ah-godit, ah-godit!*
translation- What a baseball player might say.

AH-GODUM (ah-GA-dum) Where yo shoes? (*ansr.*) *Ah-godum* inna car!
translation- I've got them... *or-* I have them in the car. (*also see* GODUM)

AH-GODDA bigo corn on my little toe on my leff foot!

AH-GOTCHA (ah-GOT-CHA) ***ah-gotcha*** that time!
translation- I've got you... Maybe after playing a joke...
Also something you might say when playing "hide n seek" with a child.
(*also see* GOTCHA)

AH-GOTCHO (ah-GOT-cho) Don't worry, *ah-gotcho* back!
   or-Ah-gotcho keys in my pocket.
   translation- I've got your... *or-* Usually a
   sarcastic rebuttal like:
   "Ah-gotcho mama right here!"

AHGOTMESUM (ah-got-me-sum) *Ahgotmesum*
   peas, *ahgotmesum* corn, *ahgotmesum*
   chicken, *ahgotmesum* mashed potatoes,
   and *ahgotmesum* cornbread! Did I forget
   anything?
   translation- Self-explanatory!

AHGOTSUM (ah-got-sum) *Ahgotsum* new shoes
   for Christmas.
   translation- same as AHGOTMESUM

AH-HEHYA (AH-HEH-ya) Its time for all of us
   to get paid, noumsayin?
   (ansr.) Ah-hehya!
   translation- I hear you... I understand you...
   I read you... I understand where you're
   coming from... I agree...

AH-IYT (ah-IYT) I'll bedare at 10:00, *ah-iyt?!*
   translation- All right?... O.K?... Do we have
   an agreement? *(also see* I-IYT)

AH-IYT-NA (ah-IYT-na) **1.** *Ah-IYT-na!* I
toldju bout dat! **2.** *(When speaking to
another brotha on the street, you may say):*
AH-IYT-NA!
translation- **1.** ALRIGHT NOW, I told you
about that. **2.** Hello.

AHN (ann) He ain't got *ahn* bidda sense!
or- **Ahn** beats nan!
translation- AHN bit of sense, is just a tiny
bit more than NAN bit of sense, which
means NONE. *(see* NAN)

AH-NO! (AH-NO!) *When you know something
emphatically.* - Yo man, you know you gotta
be here at six, and you can't be late. *You say
loud and mad-* **AH-NO!**
translation- I know. (you knew that)

AH-ODDA (AH-odd-da) *Ah-odda* smack you
inna mouth fadat!
translation- I ought to...

AH-ONBE (AH-oun-be) *Ah-ounbe* messin wit
dat stuff!
translation- I don't be... *alt.eng.-* I do not,
and would not, involve myself in the
ingestion of the aforementioned substances.

AH-ONNO (AH-on-no!) - If you don't know, and
you're upset about it.
(ah-ON-no) - If you just don't know.
(ah-ON-NO) -If you don't know, and
you don't care.
(ah-on-NO) - If you don't know, but
you are open to
suggestions.
(AH-on-NO)- If you don't know, and
are desperate for
someone to tell you.

AH-OUNT (AH-ount) Anybody want any mo
deez pokchops? (*ansr.*) *Ah-ount!*
translation- I don't.

AH-OUNWANNA (AH-oun-WAN-na)
Ah-ounwanna be here all day!
translation- I don't want to ...

AH-OUNWANT (AH-oun-WANT) *Ah-ounwant*
nomo dem beans!
translation- I don't want... (and u know why)
(*also see* NOMO)

AHSDA (AAHS-da) *Ahsda* only one that showed
up to Yomama's house for dinner.
translation- I was the... (*see* YOMAMA)

AHSLIKE (AAHS-like) When I walked in the
   door and saw what was going on, *aslike*,
   ya'll gotta be kiddin!
   translation- I was like... (*meaning*) A state
   of mind, or a state of being.

AH-UNNA (AH-un-na) *Ah-unna* git me
   somadat!
   translation- I wanna... *or*- I want to...
   alt. eng.- I wish to acquire a little of that.

AHZABOUTA (AH-za-bout-ta*) Ahzabouta* leave,
   fo you showed up.
   translation- I was about to...
   (*also see* IYSABOU-T)

AIN'T (ain't) **1.** *Ain't,* ain't in the dictionary.
   2. OH, no you *ain't* bringin
   allat stuff in here!
   translation- **1.** Ain't, ISN'T in the dictionary.
   (Cept for dis one!)   **2.** You still AIN'T
   bringin allat stuff in here!

AINATE (ain-NATE) I gotta get somethin to eat,
   I *ainate* since this moanin.
   or- What, you *ainate* chyet?
   translation- Ain't eat...
   alt. eng.- I'm famished, I haven't eaten since
   this morning.

AINEE (AIN-nee) *down south ebncs.-* **1.** We goin over to *Ainee's* house for dinner this weekend. **2.** *Ainee* the same one we saw the other day, pushing that basket?
translation- **1.** Aunt or- Auntie (one of your parent's sisters) **2.** Ain't he... Isn't he...

AINEVA (ain-NEV-va) *ebncs.-* Ah *aineva* eatin at this place again! *or-* You *aineva* lied.
translation- Ain't never... Am not ever... Won't ever... Won't again... Never...

AINONE (AIN-none) Can I please get a couple mo dem chicken wangs? (*ansr.*) Naw, cause *ainone* left.
translation- Ain't none... There aren't any... Dey all gone!

ALLA (ALL-la) *Alla* money daygot, and they don't wanna help nobody?
translation- All of the...

ALLAT (all-LAT) **1.** You spent *allat* time in there, and that's all you got done? *or-*
2. She ain't *allat!*
translation- **1.** All of that.
2. *alt.eng.-* She isn't all of what you, or she, thinks she is.

ALLAVUS (ALL-la-vus) *Allavus* are invited to a
   party at Ray-Ray's house.
   translation- You, me, ALL OF US.
   (*also see* ALLUS)

ALLEEZ (ALL-leez) Lookid *alleez* dirty dishes
   you left last night!
   translation- All of these ... (so get busy!)

ALLIM (ALL-lim) **1.** Later for *allim* fools! *or-* I want you to pickup *allim* toys and pudem up now!
translation- All of them.
alt. eng.- **1.** I think we should forget about all of those strange people.

ALLISS (ALL-liss) You get *alliss* for a dollar-fidy? *or-* You mean *alliss* time I cudda hadda V-8?
translation- All of this.

ALLKINA (all-KINE-na) We had *allkina* fun last night! *or-* We went to Uncle Joe's house for dinner last night, they had *allkina* food there!
translation- All kinds of... a variety of... many different kinds of... A whole lodda...

ALLUBM (ALL-lub-mm) Which one you wont? *(ansr.)* I want *allubm.*
translation- I would like to have ALL OF THEM. *(same as ALLUVUM)*

ALLUS (ALL-lus) When we finish playin, they goun take *allus* to dinner.
translation- All of us. *(also see ALLAVUS)*

ALLUVUM (ALL-luv-vum) *Same as* ALLUBM, but maybe a tadd more "proper."

AMABE (AM-ma-be) *Amabe* ready in about 10 minutes.
translation- I am going to be...
(*also see* AMBE *and* AMOBE)

AMABOUTA (am-ma-BOU-ta) **1.** *Amabouta* get me a raise on this new job!
2. *Amabouta* cash!
translation- **1.** I am about to...
2. I am about the... (Which means, "I get paid for what I do")

AMAHATA (HAT-ta) *Amahata* get me somadat!
translation- I'm gonna have to... I am going to have to...

AMALAMS (AM-ma-lams) *down south ebncs.-* Mama got sick, so we called the *Amalams!*
translation- Mother fell ill so we called for an AMBULANCE!

AMBE (AM-be) *Ambe* pissed if you don't call me right back!
translation- I am going to be... (As you can tell, it's a little different from AMABE)

AMBOUT (AM-bout) *Ambout* rehta go.
or- *Ambout* two seconds from yo ass!
translation- I am about...

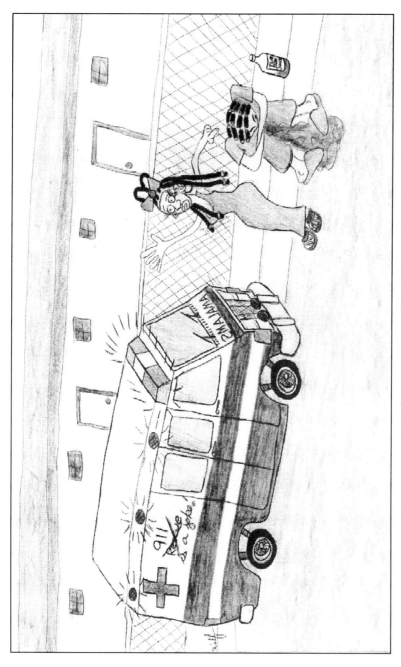

Mama got sick, so we called the *Amalams!*

AMBOUTA (am-BOUT-ta) *Ambouta* get paid!
translation- I am about to...

AMIZ (AM-miz) Whose goin to the movies?
(*ansr.*) *Amiz!*
translation- I am... *or-* I is... (What ever
seems right for you.)

AMMA (AM-ma) *Amma* git that TV set from
Rita when she moves.
translation- Same as AMO, but not as mad.

AMO (AM-mo) *Amo* smack you in yo mouth, you
keep it up!
translation- I am going to...

AMOBE (AM-mo-be) *Amobe* rollin by the endada
week!
translation- I am going to be... (the "MO"
makes it more emphatic than AMABE or
AMBE) (*also see* ROLLIN)

 ANA (an-nuh) I went and got me a pair of boots
ana hat for alliss rain!
translation- And a...

ANAMUGG (an-na-MUGG) I was lost *anamugg*
lookin for this street!
translation- (*see* AZAMUGG)
(*also see* MUGG *and* MUHFUH)

ANDUH (an-duh) *Anduh* one, *Anduh* two...
translation- Something a bandleader might
say to get the band started.

ANFERNEY HARDAWAY (ANN-fer-ny HAR-dah-way) I think his momma meant to say AnTHONy. (We could be wrong)

AN-NUH-UH (an-nuh-uh) Who was you hangin out with last nite? (*ansr.*) Well, I was with Mike, Russ, Tee, *an-nuh-uh...*
translation- Something to say when you can't think of what you WANT to say next, or you DON'T WANT to say what you're GOING to say next.
(*also see* BUTUH, UHRUH *and* UH-RUMM)

ANUHTHUN (an-NUH-thun) *Anuhthun* bites the dust.
translation- Another one... (u know the rest)...

ARTHUR RYDIS (ART-thur RYE-dis) I would help you move that refrigerator in here but, my *arthur rydis* just showed up.
translation- Arthritis... Something you'd say when your friend pulls up in his truck with that king size refrigerator you just bought from him for $25 because he needed the money.

ASSIM (ASS-sim) *Assim* if he wanna eat now or later.
translation- Ask him. (*also see* ASTIM)

ASSUM (ASS-sum) If you wanna know, go *assum!*
translation- If you would like to know the answer, you have to go and ASK THEM!

ASSUR (ASS-sur) Amma *assur* for her phone number.
translation- Ask her.

ASTER (ASS-ter) If you wanted her to go out with you last night, you shudda *aster.*
translation- Asked her.

ASTIM (ASS-tim) When I *astim* what time it was, he said it was "Nation Time" *
translation- Asked Him. (* From the '60s Black Power days. *Meaning,* The Black Nation) (*also see* ASSIM)

AUM (aum) *Aum* ready ta eat!
translation- (as if you need one) I am...

AYASS (AAAH-yass) (different from Ass) Dat girl gotsum *ayass* on her!
translation- Ass, is a normal butt. AYASS, is a very large pretty butt!
(It's a Black Man thang!)

AZAMUGG (ah-zah-MUGG) Aum hungry *azamugg! or-* It's hot *azamugg* in here!
translation- As a mugg... (you have to look up MUGG to understand this one!)

B

Take yo *BEHFOOT* self back inna house!

B

BAD-BOYS (bad-boys) *ebncs.-* How much you pay fadem *bad-boys!*
translation- Anything (shoes, tires, wheels, garden tools, condoms, etc,) that you think is kinda hip, and has some usefulness.

BAFF (baaaff) You gotta take a *baff* fo you go to bed!
translation- Bath

BAFFROOM (BAA-froom) I gotta go to the *baffroom!* *or-* Where da *baffroom* at?
translation- Zackly what it sounds like.

BAHTHOOM (BAAH-thoom) *translation-* Another attempt to say BATHROOM. (*see* BAFFROOM)

BAKADA (BAK-kuh-duh) I think I dropped my keys in *bakada* couch.
translation- Back of the...

BANK (bank) Yo man, you see homie over there? He got big *bank!*
translation- This means MONEY. (and it doesn't have to be in the bank)

BEDDERNAT (bed-dern-NAT) I can do
beddernat!
translation- Better...than...that.

BEDONE (BE-done) I *bedone* went upside his
head if I saw him do that!
translation- Be done...Will do... *or-* Would
have already done (given the circumstances).

BEENDONE (BEEN-done) Ah *beendone* nudat!
translation / alt. eng.- I knew that a LONG
TIME AGO!

BEEYACH (bee-YACH) *translation-* Something
you call someone when you are very mad,
upset, angry, disappointed, or just plain ole
pissed off with them. It's an extended
version of the word BITCH! And in this
case, it doesn't matter if it's a man or a
woman!

BEEZ (Beez) It *beez* like that sometimes. *or-* It
beez dat way!
translation- Is like... (*also see* BELIKE)

BEHFEET (BEH-feet) Don't come in here witcho
behfeet, go put some shoes on.
translation- BARE feet...

BEHFOOT (BEH-foot) Take yo *behfoot* self back inna house!
translation- And put some shoes on!

BELIKE (BE-like) **1.** Sometimes it *belike* that. **2.** Everytime I see her, I *belike*, odda my mind!
translation- **1.** Is like... *or-* That's the way it is. **2.** Am like...
alt. eng.- Whenever I see her, she puts me in a wonderful state of mind!

BET (BET) You goun meet me at 10? *Bet!*
translation- An agreement... You can bet on it.

BETBE (BET-be) You *betbe* ready when I get there!
translation- Better be...

BETCHA (BET-cha) Ah *betcha* any money, she won't be ready when we get there!
translation- Bet ya... *or-* Bet you...

BETNOT (bet-not) You *betnot* do that again!
translation- Better not. *or-* It's best NOT to...

BIDDA (BID-da) Lehme get a lil *bidda* dat sauce on deez ribs.
translation- Bit of...

BIDNE (BID-neh) Nonya *bidne!* *or-* Ahgotsum *bidne* over there!
> *translation-* Business *alt. eng.-* This is not your concern. *or-* I have some BUSINESS to take care of over there.

BIGGERNAT (BIG-gern-NAT) Ah got somethin *biggernat!*
> *translation-* Bigger than that. (What? your forehead?!)

BIGGO (BIG-go) **1.** Rodney came home wit a *biggo* knot on his head! *or-*
> **2.** Mama! I just saw a *biggo* rat downstairs in the corner!
> *translation-* **1.** Rodney came in the house with a VERY LARGE bump on his forehead!
> **2.** That rat was LARGE, and ugly too!

BIGMOMMA (BIG-mom-ma) *translation-* What
some Black folks refer to Grandmother as.
(*also see* MUDEAR)

BITE (bite) Why you tryin to *bite* my beats?
translation- What one rapper, or DJ may say
to another rapper or DJ who is trying to
copy his style.

BLEEDAT (blee-dat) You *bleedat?* *or-* Ah
bleedat when I seedat!
translation- Do you BELIEVE THAT?

BLEEDIS (blee-dis) Ah-ount *bleedis!*
translation - I don't BELIEVE THIS is what
I'm seeing!

BLEEV (BLEE-v) I do *bleev* she's married.
translation- Believe. (So step off!)

BODAVAS (BO-da-vas) They called and said
they wanted *bodavas* to come.
translation- Both of us...
(*also see* DABODAVAS)

BOFDEM (BOF-dem) I'd git in *bofdem* fools asses if dey came to me wit dat! *translation / alt. eng.-* I would have to punish BOTH OF THEM, if they came in here with any foolishness!

BOFUM (BOF-fum) Which one you want? *(ansr.)* I want *bofum*. *translation-* I would like to have BOTH OF THEM, thank you.

BOFUS (BO-fuss) Momma wants *bofus* to comina house. *translation-* Both of us...

BOFYALL (BOF-yall) I want *bofyall* to go to bed right now. *translation-* Both of you. (*also see* DABODAYOUS)

BOOGAH (BOOG-gah) (not booGER) Shssss, (*whispering*) Hey man, you got a *boogah* hangin outcha nose. *or-* Yo man, waounchu wipe dat *boogah* offya nose! *translation-* self explanatory

BOOYAAH (BOO-yaah) *translation-* A sound we use to describe many things, like the sound of a gun, or 40dd's bustin out of a 36c bra. (*also see* TA-DOW)

BOSTA (BO-sta) You *bosta* have a driver's license to drive a car.
translation- Suppose to... (*also see* POSTA)

BOUTCHO (BOUT-cho) Hey man, they over there talkin *boutcho* mama!
translation- About Your... (shoes... clothes... car... haircut... wife... etc..)
(*also see* ABOUTCHO)

BREAK-OFF (break-off) Don't worry, when I get mine, I'll *breakoff* a lil som-in for all ya'll.
or- (break-me-off) I know you can *breakmeoff* a little piece.
or- (break-u-off) For being in my corner so strong, Ama *breakuoff* a good pisa dis!
translation- TO SHARE...

BREFF (breff) Girl, yo *breff* smell like sweet buttermilk!
translation- An "Old School" brotha tryin to rap to a young lady by telling her how nice her BREATH smells.

BROHAMM (bro-ham) (*same as* BROSKEE)

BROSKEE (bro-ski) *translation-* Another word for brother... friend... homey... good buddy... pal... good guy...

BROTHA (BRA-the) (not bro-THER) Wussup ma ***brotha?!***
translation- One of the things we refer to Black Men as.

BUGGIN (BUG-gin) Shebe ***buggin*** every time she sees him lookin at another woman.
translation- Bugging out... going crazy... having uncontrollable anger... get a life! (*also see* WIGGIN)

BUDDA (BUH-duh) Pass the ***budda*** please.
translation- Would you please pass the BUTTER?

BUMPIN (BUMP-pin) We was kinda ***bumpin*** last night.
translation- Dancing... Groovin hard... Havin a good time... What ever we were doing, we wuz doing it good!

BUNCHA (BUN-cha) Dat ain't nothin but a ***buncha*** mess!
translation- A bunch of...

BUSA (BUS-sa) **1.** You say you a rapper, lehme hear you *busa* rhyme.
   2. We can't sit here all day, we gon hatuh *busa* move.
   3. You don't pay me my money, ama hatuh *busa* cap inyo ass!
   translation- **1.** Something a rapper does...
   2. Make a move on... Leave... **3.** Shoot you!

BUTCHU (but-CHU) **1.** Ah ain't sleepin wit nobody *butchu!* *or-* **2.** I wanted to come here at 7, *butchu* said to be here at 6.
   translation- **1.** But you... *as in* - Only you. (*Something one spouse says to the other untrusting spouse.*) **2.** But you...
   as in- But you...

BUTUH (but-tuhhh) I was gonna pay you back yesterday, *butuh...*
   translation- Something to say, BEFORE you say, what you DON'T KNOW you're GOING to say! (*also see* AN-NUH-UH, UHRUH, *and* UHRUMM)

BUTUH-RUHH (but-tuhh-ruhhh) *same as* BUTUH, *but with a little more contemplation.*

Pass the *budda* please.

BZZOMB! (BZZ-zomb) Yo man, the club last night
was the *bzzomb!*
translation / alt. eng.- We went to the club
last night and had a really, really great
time!

C

Whachyall-doin? (*ansr.*) ***Chillin***.

C

CATTIE-BITCH (KAAH-tee BITCH) Cattie-like
a cat... Bitch-like a BITCH
translation- A woman (or better yet, a
BITCH) who participates in activities such
as: **1.** Blatantly looking another woman up
and down, while she's with her man,
looking as if she's saying, "What is SHE
doing with HIM?!"... **2.** Purposely, and
maliciously, disrespecting another woman
by flirting with her man right in her face...
3. One who will call a man's house, and if a
woman answers the phone, she will not
acknowledge, or respect the presence of that
woman, whether she knows who that
woman is or not...

CAV (kaav) *Cav* wonnym?
translation- Can I have? *alt. eng.-* May I
have one of those?

CEPT (cept) Everything's cool, *cept* for one thing.
translation- Ebonic for: Except.

CHANAMIS? (cha-NAME-is) *Chanamis?*
translation- Your name is? *or-* What is your
name?

CHASS (chass) Sit *chass* down! *or-* Get *chass*
   back in the house now!
   translation- Your Ass...

CHECOT (CHEK-cot) Yo man, *checot* dem shoes
   she got on.
   translation- Check out... *or-* (*in this case*)
   To look at.

CHEKIDOT (che-ki-DOT) **1.** Yo man, *chekidot*,
   I got $5.00 on some BBQ. *or-* **2.** That club
   looks like its bumpin, lets *chekidot!*
   (*see* BUMPIN)
   translation- Check it out... **1.** To understand.
   2. To investigate.

CHIGONADU (chi-GON-na-DU) *"CHIGONADU*
   WHEN THEY COME FOR YOU?"
   (song from some cop t.v. show)
   translation- What are you going to do?...

CHIGONDU (chi-GON-du) *Chigondu* boutcho
   car? *or- Chigondu* tonite?
   translation- Same as CHIGONADU without
   the "GONA".
   (*Also see* WHACHU-GONDU)

CHILLIN (CHILL-lin) **1.** Whachyall-doin? (*ansr.*) *Chillin.* or- **2.** (*a real down south thing*) Is dat dem *chillin* from cross da street?
translation.- **1.** Coolin out... relaxing... (*also see* KIKINIT) **2.** Children (you knew that)

CHIREN (CHEER-ren) *The nice little old lady from across the street stands on her front porch and says:* I just love to see all the little *chiren* playin outside!
translation- CHILDREN (Cuz dey won't be in here tearin up the house!)

CHO (cho) Sit *cho* ass down!
translation- YOUR
alt. eng. - Please take a seat.

CHUDUWIN? (chew-DU-win *or-* CHU-du-win) *Chuduwin* in here?
translation- What are you doing?

CHULOOKINAT (CHU-look-kin-at-?)
Chulookinat?
translation- What are YOU looking at?

CHUWANNA (chew-WAN-na) **1.** *Chuwanna* do tonight?
or just- **2.** *CHUWANNA* DO?!!
translation- **1.** What do you want to do tonight?
2. Something you might say just before a fight.

CHUWONT? (chew-WONT) *Chuwont?*
   translation- What do you want?

CHYALL (chy'ALL) **1.** *Chyall* doin? *or-* *Chyall*
   taunmot? **2.** *Chyall* wanna eat?
   translation- **1.** What are you all doing? *or-*
   talking about? **2.** What do you all want to
   eat? (*also see* WHACHYALL)

CHYET (chyet) Yall ain't eat *chyet*?
   translation- This is a "Yet" that comes after
   a word that ends with a "T" sound.

CLUBIN (KLUH-been) Webe *clubin!*
   (*Something I heard some six graders at an
   elementary school graduation party say.*)
   translation- Clubing... Going out to clubs...
   Having a good time in clubs... Party'n like
   we're in a club!...

C'MOUN (ca-MOUN) *C'moun* nah, you gotta do
   better'n nat! *or-* Will you *c'moun*, we late!
   translation- Come on...

COMINA (COME-men-na) I wount chu, and yo
   lil brotha ta *comina* house.
   translation- Come in the...

CONA (CONE-na) The stoe is rouna *cona*.
translation / alt. eng.- To git to the store,
you have to go around the CORNER.

CONVASATE (CON-va-sate) You think you
smart enough to *convasate* wit me?
translation- Huh, maybe not. (smirk)

COODIES (COO-deez) *This is some old school
youngster ebncs.*- I don't want none if you
got your *coodies* on it.
translation- Coodies - Little invisible germ
looking things that you get when people
don't like you.

COOLINOUT (coo-lin-OUT) Man, aum just here
at home, *coolinout.*
translation- In the process of chillin... Or,
(for you proper folks) just resting.

COOLOUT (coo-LOUT) Man, afta last night, I
think aum just gone *coolout.*
translation- Chillout... relax... take it
easy... stay out of trouble...

COP (cop) When I get paid, the first thang amo do
is *cop* me a pair uhdim green shoes I saw
inna mall yestiday.
translation- To buy

Everytime I sleep witchu, u-b takin all the *covah!*

COVAH (COV-va) *translation-* Cover... blanket... spread...

CRACKIN (CRACK-kin) What's *crackin*?! *translation-* What's going on?... What's happening?

CRIB (crib) She got a nice *crib.* *translation-* House... apartment... place where you live...

CRONIC (CRON-nic) Lehme just hit a little bit o this *cronic,* and Ah be good ta go.
translation- Smoke... Bud... Marijuana... Splive... Blunt... etc... JUST SAY NO!

CUPLA (CUP-la) I need one of these, one of those, and a *cupla* dem.
translation- A couple of...
OR-
CUPLIM (cup-PLIM) I could use a *cuplim* chicken wangs right about now!
translation- A couple of them...

CUZ (cuz) **1.** Wussup *cuz?!* **2.** I didn't do it yesterday *cuz* you said you was gonna do it today.
translation - **1.** Cousin, homeboy, friend, naybahood mate... **2.** BECAUSE.

D

DAREDIZ! Ah been lookin all over fadat!

D

DABEEN (duh-been) Ah *dabeen*... He *dabeen*... She *dabeen*... We *dabeen* rich by now if it wasn't fuhduh dog eatin up the lottery tickets!
translation- Would have been...

DABENJAMINS (da-BEN-jah-mins) Aum just stackin up *dabenjamins* so I can cop dat crib I been checkin out.
translation- One Hundred-Dollar Bills.

DABODAVUS (da-BO-da-vas) Ah got a lil somethin for *dabodavus!*
translation- The both of us...
(*also see* BODAVAS)

DABODAYOUS (da-BO-da-youss) I ain't just talkin to one of yous, aum talkin to *dabodayous!*
translation- The both of you.

DA-BOMB (da-BOMB) *ebncs.*- Yo man, that jamy last nite was *da-bomb!*
translation- Very very good!... Great...
alt.eng.- We had a fantastic time last night!

DADDUH (DAD-duh) **1.** Ain't *dadduh* bitch!
2. *Dadduh* be the day. **3.** Is *dadduh* new
shirt?
translation- **1.** This is one that everyone
uses. I guess one of the meanings could be-
"Now isn't that something!" **2.** THAT WILL
be the day. **3.** Is THAT A...

DAGONNIT (DAAH-gon-nit) *Dagonnit,* I knew I
shuda donnit yesterday.
translation- A substitute for Got Dammit!

DAHOOD (da-HOOD) We in *dahood* now ya'll!
or- I live in *dahood.*
translation- A proud place of residence...
Short for neighborhood
(*also see* NAYBAHOOD)

DANE (DAI'ne) You said you were going to pay
me $50 last week. (*response*) *Dane* what I
said!
translation- That ain't... that isn't...
alt. eng.- You have mistaken, THAT IS NOT
what I said!

48

DANG (dang) Aw momma, *dang!* Just when
we're starting to have fun, you makin us
comina house.
translation- Something kids say before
they're old enough to use the word DAMN.
(Which if they used DANG too much is
going to get them a serious butt whuppin
anyway!)

DAREDIZ (DARE-diz) *Darediz!* Ah been lookin
all over fadat!
translation- There it is.

DAS (das) *"DAS* THE WAY, uh-huh uh-huh, I
LIKE IT"
translation- That's...

DASHACUM (DAS-ha-cum) *Dashacum* we came
to this place, insteada goin to that other
place. *or-* He hit me! *Dashacum* I socked
him the nose, punched him in the stomach,
and talked about his mama!
translation- That's how come... That's why...

DASHIT (da-SHIT!) Now, that's *dashit!*
translation- A term we use to describe some
of the greatest things in life!

DASRITE (das-RITE) *Dasrite*, I ain't takin no
more of your stuff!
translation- THAT'S RIGHT, you don't have to.

DASSA (DAS-sa) *Dassa* nice car she's drivin.
or- Dassa badd muhfuh!
translation- That's a...

DASSIT (DAS-sit) *Dassit*, das what am
taunmot!
translation- THAT'S IT, that's what I'm
talking about!

DASUM (DAS-sum) *Dasum* bull s___!
translation- That's some... (u-no da rest)

DASWUT (DAS-wut) *Daswut* ah said! *or-*
Daswut aum taunmot!
translation- THAT'S WHAT I said, and
THAT'S WHAT I'm... (u-no duh rest)

DAT (dat) Gimme *dat!* *or-* Das *dat* mugg
overdare!
translation- That...
alt.eng.- There's the person I was speaking of.

DATBE-IT (DAT-b-it) *At a drive thru restaurant, the person inside would say over the
speaker-* Would you like anything else? *And
you say-* Naw, **Datbe-it!**
translation- (if you really need one) That
will be it.

DAUDA (DAU-da) My brotha has four **dauda's**
and a son. *or-* You bedder stay away from
my **dauda!**
translation- Daughter

DEEZ (deez) Whose sox are **deez?**
translation- These

DEFF (deff) U-gon watch **DEFF** COMIDY JAM
tonight? *or-* Those shoes are **deff!**
translation- Something real good...
Happening... Fantastic... DEFFintely dashit!

DEH (deh) **1. Deh** told me you wuddn't goun be
here today. **2. "DEH**-O!..."
Translation 1. They... 2. "Daylite come and
me wanna go home"

DEHBE (DEH-be) **Dehbe** acting funny over
there.
translation- They be.... *alt. eng.-* Their
behavior is very strange.

DEH-HEGO (DEH-he-go) You lookin for Ruben? *Deh-hego!*
translation- There he goes...

DEH-HEIZZ (DEH-he-izz) Yeah, I see him. *Deh-heizz* right dare.
translation- There he is...

DEHSUM (DEH-sum) *Dehsum* chicken in the icebox.
translation- THERE IS SOME chicken in the refrigerator.

DEHWAZ (DEH-waz) **1.** *Dehwaz* 4 or 5 ofvum there fo I left.
2. *Dehwaz* hollern an screamin fo YOU came home!
translation- **1.** There was... *or-* There were... **2.** They was... *or-* They were...

DEHZA (DEH-za) *Dehza* man at the doe!
translation- THERE IS A gentleman at the front door.

DEM (DIM) Tell *dem* fools to be quiet!
translation- Them

DEN (din) First we goin to the movies, *den* we gon get son-in to eat. *or-* I-iyt *den.*
translation- Then (*also see* I-IYTDEN)

DEY (day) *Dey* told us *dey* didn't need us.
   translation- They

DEYGOT (dey-got) *Deygot* a whole lotta food on
   the menu. *or-* "*DEYGOT*
   CRAZY LITTLE WOMEN THERE....
   "(some Kansas City song)
   translation- They got...

When it come to cookin, Aum the best *DEYIS!*

DEYIS (day-IS) Aum the best *deyis!*
    translation- I am the best THERE IS.

DIBS (dibs) I got *dibs* on the last drumstick!
    translation- I have self proclaimed rights
    to...

DIDJU (did-JU) *Didju* do your homework yet?
    or- Didju eat fo you came here?
    translation- Did you?

DIH'N (DIH-n) Oh no she *dih'n* wear that green
    dress wit that red weave, orange lipstick,
    brown fishnet stockings, and house shoes to
    my party!
    translation- Didn't... (And yes she did, wit
    her rainbow lookin butt!)

DINCHU (DIN-chu) *Dinchu* know we had to be
    here at six?
    translation- Well, DIDN'T YOU?...

DISCO (DISS-co) Where *disco*?
    translation- Where does THIS GO? (U
    thought we was talkin bout a club huh?!)

DISMUCH (dis-much) Yo man, gimmie *dismuch!*
    translation- This much... *also-* When you
    hold your arm straight out with your fist
    clenched to indicate the space you would
    like between you and the another person.
    (Which is another word for "arm's length")

DISS (diss) **1.** Oh, now you gonna *diss* me!
2. You want *diss?*
translation- **1.** To disrespect **2.** This...

DISSN (DIS- sin) **1.** If you keep *dissn* people,
You WILL get dissed the way you been
dissn, but much worse! **2.** Gimme *dissn,*
dissn, and dat one.
translation- **1.** Disrespecting...
2. This one...

DIYAM (DEE-yam) When you see something
amazing, you say: *Diyam!*
translation- Damn...
alt. eng.- Oh my goodness!

DOE (doe) "OPEN THE *DOE* RICHARD!"
translation- Door

DOG (dog) Wassup *dog!?*
translation- Another word for- homeboy...
homie... cuz... ma nigga... my friend...
my buddy... my pal...

DON-NARE (don-nare) Whachyall doin *don-*
nare?
translation- Down there...
(same as DOWNAR)

DONNIT (DONE-nit) You know you shoulda *donnit* yesterday! *or-* Who *donnit?*
translation- Done it...

DOODAT (DO-dat) **1.** I told you not to *doodat*!
or- Yo man, I can *doodat!*
or- **2. *Doodat*** thang!
translation- **1.** Do that... Get it done...
2. Something you say to someone who is dancing or doin somethin real good!

DOUNCHU (DOUN-chu) You know beddernat, *dounchu?*
or- (doun-CHU) *Dounchu* look at me like that!
translation- (of course) Don't you...
(Something yo mama or daddy might say to you when you do something wrong!)

DOUNBE (DOUN-be) *Dounbe* messin with my stuff!
translation- Don't be... Do not...
alt. eng.- Please don't bother my belongings.

DOUNNO (doun-no) You *dounno* whachu doin.
or better yet- "You *dounno* your ass from a hole inna ground!"
translation- Don't know...

DOPE (dope) **1.** Yo man, that was *dope!* **2.** Got any *dope?*
translation- **1.** A situation, experience, *or* anything that is done exceptionally well... **2.** A substance you ingest that is very stupid! (That's why they call it DOPE!)

DOWN (down) **1.** So wassup? You *down* or what? **2.** That's a *down* sista!
translation- **1.** Are you in agreement... Are you participating with us? **2.** Down to earth... really cool... has her head together...

DOWNA-WAY (DOWN-na-WAY) *southern ebncs.-* The store is *downa-way.*
translation- Down the way... *or-* On the way...

DOWNAR (DOWN-nar) Chuduwin *downar?*
translation- What are you doing DOWN THERE? (*same as* DON-NARE)

DOZE (doze) *Doze* yo kids?
translation- Those... Are THOSE your kids?
alt. eng.- Are you the proud parents of those wonderful and talented children?

DUGODDA (DEW-god-da) Lisa ain't allat fine, but she ***dugodda*** nice house, a nice car, a college degree, a good heart, and a BIGGO ASS! (it's a guy thang)
translation- Do got a... does have a...

DUHFUHK (duh-FUHK) What ***duhfuhk!?*** *or-* ***Duhfuhk*** you doin in here?
or- Man, She plays ***duhfuhk*** odda that violin!
translation- The F... (exactly what it sounds like)

DUKE EDDINGTON (DUKE ED-ding-ton) Ain't dat dat old guy dat plays jazz widda buncha musicians playin allkina instruments?
translation- Something someone who is very YOUNG would say. (*HAS to be, unless they're stupid*) Duke ELLINGTON. One of America's greatest Composers, and Orchestra leaders!

E

We at the *endada* line.

E

ELAMINO-P (EL-la-min-no-P) *ebncs*- H, I, J, K,
ELAMINO-P.
translation- h-i-j-k-L-M-N-O-P (U nudat)

ENDADA (END-duh-duh) We at the *endada*
line. *or*- Ah-ount get paid til the *endada*
month.
translation- End of the...

EURF (eurf) What on *eurf* are you doing? *or*-
Didju feel that *eurf* quake?
translation- Earth

EVAH (EH-vah) Dounchu *EVAH* do that again!
translation- Ever

EVEYTHANG (EH-vee-thang) She plays drums
and *eveythang*!
translation- Something Magic Johnson said,
on the second night of his show, about
Sheila E. playing drums and EVERYTHING.

EXSREWSME (ex-SCREWS-me) *I'm sorry, but I
heard it myself. A sista from the hood,
trying to be all proper, goes into a store and
says; **Exsrewsme**, what time do you close?*
translation- You figure it out!

F

If it wudn *fadem* ants, weda had a nice picnic!

F

FADAT (fah-DAT) *ebncs.-* Ama gitchu *fadat*! *translation-* For that... *alt. eng.-* I'm going to make sure you get your just punishment for your deeds!

FADEEZ (fah-DEEZ) How much you want *fadeez?* *translation-* For these.

FADEM (fah-DEM) How much you pay *fadem* shoes? *or-* If it wudn *fadem* ants, weda had a nice picnic! *translation-* For them... *or in this case-* For those... (*see* FADOZE)

FADISS (fah-DISS) Ah paid $100 *fadiss* watch! *translation-* For this...

FADOZE (fah-DOZE) You want $500? *Fadoze?* *translation-* FOR THOSE... all ofvum... (*also see* FADEM)

FAHGITCHU (fah-GIT-chu) *Fahgitchu* if you don't wanna talk to me! *or-* Don't worry, I won't *fahgitchu. or- "Fahgitchu* , Forgotchu, Never Thought About Chu!" *translation-* Forget you... I will or will not forget about you... later for you!... *or-* F...U!

FART (fart) Ah-iyt, who *farted?*
   translation- P.U.

FEELIN (FEEL-lin) Ah ain't *feelin* him. *or-* Oh
   yeah, aum *feelinya* now!
   translation- Same as FEELYA

FEELYA (FEEL-ya) *Ah feelya!*
   translation- When you are FEELING *or-*
   NOT FEELING the SINCERITY of a
   person's speech, action, or performance.
   or, to put it simply- Be FO-REAL!

FIDNA (FID-na) Aum *fidna* get PAID!
   translation- Fixing to... about to... getting
   ready to... preparing to...
   (*also see* FINTU *and* FIXIN)

FIDY (FIH-dy) I paid a dollar-*fidy* fadeez sox.
   or- 48, 49, *FIDY!*
   translation- self explanatory

FIHDEEN (fih-DEEN) *Back stage before the band
   goes on...* How much time we got before we
   hit? (*answer*) *FIHDEEN!* (*as in minuets*)
   or- 11,12,13,14, *fihdeen.* *translation-* **15**

FINTU (FIN-tu) *same as* FIDNA

FIXIN (FIX-sin) **1.** Am *fixin* to go get somethin to eat. **2.** Am *fixin* pancakes. Want some?
translation- **1.** Getting ready to...
(*same as* FIDNA *and* FINTU)
2. Preparing... *or-* cooking...

FLAVOR (FLA-vor) Yo, what's the *flavor*?
or- Oh, I see what the *flavor* is!
translation- Mood... attitude...

FLO (flow) *southern ebncs.-* **1.** Watch whatchu doin, you droppin food all over the *flo!* *or-* It's your turn to mop the *flo* tonite. **2.** Aum feelin the *flo!*
translation- **1.** Floor **2.** Flow... *as in-* good mood... vibe... atmosphere...

FLY (fly) Yo man, yo sista's kinda *fly.*
translation- Hip... slick... dresses fashionable... great attitude... I like her!

FO (foe) **1.** I saw him day *fo* yesterday. *or-* You bedder watch out *fo* you fall.
2. 1, 2, 3, *fo.*
translation- **1.** Before... **2.** Four...

FO-INE! (FOINE) U-no Lukrisha? Dat girl is
fo-ine!

translation- You have "fine," which means
beautiful. Then you have "**fo-ine,**" which is
seriously (which means real, REAL), stupid
fine! (*see* STUPID)

FO-REAL (fo-REAL) *We all know this one...* Be for real... Be honest... Tell the truth... *BUT, check the next one...*

FO-REALDO (fo-REAL-doe) *Fo-realdo?* You gonna cut your hair, dye it green, and then twist it into tiny lil' knots? *Fo-realdo?* *translation-* For Real Though?... (*same as* FO-REAL with the DOE added)

FODY (FO-dee) When you gonna gimme that *Fody* dollars you owe me?
or- Ama go down to the likasto and git me a *fody. or-* 37, 38, 39, *fody!*
translation- 40 (*see* LIKASTO)

FOEHEAD (FOE-head) Yo *foehead's* too big fadat hat!
translation- Forehead

FOFA (FO-fa) **1.** Whachu doin *fofa* July? *or-*
2. They're on sale, *fofa* a dollar.
translation- **1.** Fourth of July **2.** Four for a dollar...

FRIGERADER (FRIG-ger-rate-der) There's some Kool-Aid in the *frigerader.*
translation- RE-frigerator
(*also see* ICEBOX)

FRONT (front) Why you tryin to *front?* or-
Don't be *front'n* like you got some money!
translation- To act like, or make others
believe you got your thing together, when
you DON'T!

FSHO (fah-SHO) *a down south ebnc. thang-* Ya'll
goin to the movies tonight? *(ansr.)*
Fsho!
translation- Yes, FOR SURE, we're going to
the movies.

F.T.D. S. *translation- FUHKTHEDUMBSHIT!*

FUHDUH (fuh-duh) How long you goun be here?
(ansr.) Ah be here *fuhduh* restada day.
or- I need smo ketchup *fuhduh* fries.
translation- For the...

FUHWUT? (fuh-WUT) Can you please tell me
whachu put in them biscuits you made last
night? *(ansr.) Fuhwut?* You kaint cook!
translation- For What?

FUHYA (FUH-ya) "AH GOT LOVE *FUHYA*
BABY" *or-* Yo Johnny, we'll wait *fuhya*...
but not too long.
translation- For You...

FUNETIC (fun-NEH-tic) This *funetic* dictionary
is kinda fun.
translation- A play on the word "Phonetic."
(the study of the SOUND of words and peech.)

G

GANGSTA (GANG-sta) *translation-* Gangster...
someone who participates in activities such
as: dope dealing... drive by's... gang banging...
disrespecting women, elders, authority, and
most people... not smiling in public... not
enjoying their life, and not wanting you to
enjoy yours... (*also see G. and O.G.*)

G

G. (gee) *ebncs.-* Wadup **G.**

> *translation-* **G.** for gangsta. *or* wannabe gangsta...
> (sometimes it's hard to tell because they're all trying to look HARD)

GANGSTA (GANG-sta) *see illustration*

GETDAFUHKADAHEH (GET-da-fuh-kah-da-heh)
Getdafuhkadaheh!
> *translation-* **1.** A response to something ridiculous, that was said, or done. It means- Aw c'mon... You gotta be kidding... Get out of here...*or-* **2.** Exactly what it sounds like- Get The Fuhk Out Of Here... leave... go somewhere else... BYE!

GID-BIZZY (gid-BIZ-zy-) 1. "LESS **GID-BIZZY!** "
> *(Arsenio Hall bonics)*
>> *or-* (gidn-BIZ-zy) **2.** Webe **gidn-bizzy**
>> winnevah we gets together!
>> *and-* (gids-BIZ-zy) **3.** Ah **gids-bizzy**
>> every time my woman comes home.
>> *(yeah, cleaning up the house)*
> *translation-* U-no u don't need one.

GIDOFF (gid-doff) **1.** Waounchu *gidoff* my back!
2. We gonna *gidoff* tonight!
translation- **1.** Get off, *as in-* Get off, *as in-*
Leave me alone! **2.** Get off, *as in-* having
fun, or doing something real, real good.
(*also see* GOTOFF)

GIDOUTMA (gid-DOUT-ma) *Gidoutma* way!...
face!... bed!... car!... house!... life!
translation- Get out of my...

GIDWITME (gid-WIT-me) When you get back in
town, u-no you godda *gidwitme*! *or just*
plain ole- **GIDWITME!**
(*Byron Miller bonics*)
translation- Get With Me... Let's hook up...
Let's get together... Call me...

GIHCHIR (gih-chir) (*more of a down south thing*)
1. What time you gonna *gihchir?* *or -* **2.**
See that flyswadder over there, *gihchir.*
translation- **1.** Git here. **2.** Give it here.

GIMME (GIM-me) **1.** *Gimme* dat! *or-*
2. "*GIMME* SOME LOVE!"
translation- **1.** Give me that! **2.** What a
performing artist might say on stage.

GITCHO (GIT-cho) *Gitcho* raggedy, need a haircut, holly jean wearin, bad breath havin, front tooth missin, what are you doing outside anyway, ass back in the house, NOW!
translation- Git your...

GITCHU (GIH-chu) Man, you better come *gitchu* soma dis food fo isall gone!
translation- Git you... *or-* Git yourself some...

GO-DA (GO-da) **1.** *Go-da* bed! *or-* *Go-da* hell! **2.** You godda *go-da* same way you came!
translation- **1.** Go to... **2.** Go the...

GODDA (GOD-da) **1.** You *godda* gitchu some money, a car, and a haircut before you try to talk to her. **2.** You *godda* big green thing stuck in between yo teef.
translation- **1.** Have got to... **2.** Got A... (*also see* GOTSTA)

GODDIT (GA-dit) He told me he *godit* yesterday!
translation- Got it.

GODDUM (GAH-dum) So you finally **goddum** huh?
translation- Got them.

GO-DUHDUH (GO-duh-duh) Ah-godda **go-duhduh** baffroom.
translation- Go to the...

GONHAFTA (gone-HAAF-ta) *a proper way of saying* GONHATA

GONHATA (gone-HAAH-ta) You **gonhata** leave me alone!
translation- Gonna have to... *or-* Going to have to... (before you get beatup)

GOODERNA (GOOD-dern-na) That food was **gooderna** mugg!
translation- Gooder Than A... *or-* Good... The food was Good!

GOODIZA (GOOD-diz-za) I was at the concert last nite. Ya'll sounded **goodiza** muhfuh!
translation- Good As A... (*see* MUHFUH)

GOTCHA (GOT-cha) **1.** *Gotcha*, didn't I?! **2.** Yo man, don't worry, we *gotcha* back! *translation-* **1.** Got you... **2.** Got your... *meaning-* We're behind you all the way. (Just don't mess up!) (*also see* AH-GOTCHA)

GOTOFF (got-OFF) Baby, you *gotoff* last night! *translation / alt. eng.-* You were WONDERFUL last night.

GOTSTA (GOT-sta) Ah *gotsta* git me sumadat! *translation-* I have GOT TO, without a doubt.

GOTTARUBBINOUN (got-tuh-RUB-bin-noun) (*you may use any combination to make this sentence work*) Afta dinner, I... she... we *gottarubbinoun* her... my... each other's stomach... leg... back... head... breast... butt. *translation-* Got to rubbing on... We was rubbin one another... *alt. eng.-* The after dinner massage was exquisite.

74

GOUN (GOUN) **1.** *Goun* witcho bad self!
2. *Goun* over there and say hello.
3. You *goun* do what I told ju to do!
translation- **1.** Go On... *alt. eng.-* You've
done very well for yourself, I'm proud of you!
2. Go on over there... **3.** Gonna *or-*
Going to do...

GOUNBE (goun-be) We *gounbe* i-iyt soon as my
income comes in.
translation- Gonna be... *or-* Going to be...

GOUNDU (goun-do) **1.** Whachu *goundu?* *or-*
2. Chyall *goundu* bout dem roaches?
translation- **1.** Gonna do... **2.** What are you
all going to do?

GOUNIN (GOUN-nin) **1.** If you don't wanna stay
wit us, *gounin!* **2.** *Gounin,* make yoself at
home!
translation- **1.** Go on then ...(*meaning*)
Leave! **2.** Go On IN...

GOUNOUN (goun-NOUN) **1.** Wus *gounoun?*
2. U-no dat girl goddit *gounoun!*
translation- **1.** What's GOING ON?...
What's happening?... Ha-yall doin?
2. Has got it GOING ON... has her thing
together... is kinda cute... I like her!

GOWINOUT (go-win-NOUT) I ain't *gowinout* like dat!
  translation- Going out... *as in-* Finishing up a situation in a bad way, and being embarrassed about it... Losing out and feeling bad about it...
  alt. eng.- I will not compromise my integrity by lowering my ethical, and moral principles to the level of hostile retaliation.

GREEZIN (GREE-zin) Webe *greezin* every time we go to that waffle-chicken joint!
  translation- Eating... enjoying a hearty meal... (*same as* GRUBBIN)

GREEZY (GREE-zee) Go wipe dem *greezy* lips.
  or- Dat chicken is too *greezy!*
  translation- greasy or oily

GRIP (grip) Man, I won a *grip* of money at the track yesterday!
  translation- A whole handful of... which means, a whole lot of....

GRUBBIN (GRUB-bin) Webe *gubbin* every time we go to that chicken-waffle joint!
  translation- Eating... enjoying a hearty meal... (*same as* GREEZIN)

GRUBBOUN (GRUB-bone) *As a Black man at an "all-u-can-eat" restaurant walks back to his table with food piled so high on his plate, you can't see his face, the response from his girlfriend is-* Oh, I see you seriously fidna get yo **grubboun!**
translation- GRUB (*as in-* food... appetite...) ON (*as in-* LETS EAT!)

G.T.F.O. *translation-* Get The Fuhk Out!

GUBMENT (GUB-ment) Am waitin on my **gubment** check. *or-* Ama go donare and git me somadat **gubment** cheese!
translation- Government... Also, another word for welfare check and food stamps.

H

I paid a *HUNNED* dollars fadem tires.

H

HADAHELLAHYA (HA-da-hell-LAH-ya) *ebncs.-*
Ah ain't seen you in a long time,
hadahellahya?
translation- How the hell are you? How
have you been doing?

HAISOMEVA (HA-is-some-EV-va) *a country*
person trying to properly say- HOWEVER.

HA-UNO (1. HA-you-no *or-* 2. ha-YOU- no)
1. *Ha-uno* if you ain't nevah seen one? *or-*
2. *Ha-Uno* what she said if you ain't never
talked to her?
translation- How do you know?

HAYAM! (HAY-yam) *Hayam*, that girl is fine!
(*We usually pronounce it with an H around*
respectable people, like...Parents.)
translation- A replacement for "Dayam!"
Which is a replacement for "Damn!" Which
is a replacement for "Oh my goodness!"

HEBE (he-be) Everytime he comes around, *hebe*
tryin to hug all the women.
translation- He is... He is being... He does...
or- is doing

HEH'GO (heh-GO) "LIKE TO HEAR IT?,
HEH'GO! " *or-* Yo man, *heh'go* that $3.00 I
owe you.
translation- here it goes... here it is..

HISSASS (HIS-sass) **1.** *Hissass* is mine!
2. Amo buss *hissass!*
translation / alt. eng.- **1.** I am going to get
even with him when I see him. **2.** I am
going to have to punish him to the N'th
(*maximum*) degree.

HIZNN (HIZ-zin) *country ebncs.-* Dis one's yourn,
dat one's *hiznn*
translation- His... This one is yours, that
one IS HIS.

HODON (hoe-don) Wait, *hodon* a minute.
translation- Hold on. (*also see* HOLLON)

HOE (hoe) I know dat *hoe*! *or-* Wareda *hoes* at?
translation- A very derogatory term used
(unfortunately) to describe certain women.
(Unless they act like it)

HOLDUP (hole-dup) Naw, naw, *holdup!* We
goundu what?
translation- Wait a minute.
(*also see* HOLLUP)

HOLLER (HA-ler) Tee, lehme *holler* atcha for a minute.
translation- Speak to... *alt. eng.*- Terrence, may I indulge a moment of your time, so that I may have a word with you?

HOLLON (hole-LON) Yo, yo, yo, *hollon*, lehme talk to you for a minute.
translation- A guy trying to get a young lady to HOLD ON (or wait), so he can rap to her. (*same as* HODON)

HOLLUP (hole-LUP) *Hollup, hollup*!
translation- same as HOLDUP without the "DUP" (*see* HOLDUP)

HOMEBOYEE (HOME-boy-ee) *translation*- Someone from my block, neighborhood, part of town, city, state, country, etc.

HOMIE (HOME-mee) Das my *homie* ovadare!
translation- Same as HOMEBOYEE

HOOCHIE (HOO-chie) **1.** Why u-b wearin them *hoochie* mama dresses to church? **2.** That woman next door got them lil 5 and 6 year old kids dancin them *hoochie* dances at their birthday parties.
translation- **1.** A dress that a person who dances in a strip club might wear.
2. A dance that a person who dances in a strip club might do.

HOOCHIE-MAMA (HOO-chie mom-ma) Tell yo
hoochie-mama girl friend dounbe callin
my house nomo! (*something your mother, or
wife might say*)
translation- A woman who looks like, acts
like, and dresses like she dances in a strip
club. (And probably does!)

HOOKMEUP (hook-me-up) **1.** Yo man, wyounchu
hookmeup wit her friend? *or-* **2.** Man, can
you *hookmeup* wit a playduhdat food?
(see PLAYDUHDAT)
translation- **1.** Turn me on to... Introduce
me to... **2.** Give me, (as a favor)...

HOOPDEE (HOOP-dee) *translation-* A big, long,
old, ugly, raggedy ass, car that we used to
drive back in the '60s, '70s and 80's to get
from point A, to point B.
(It also doubled as a dressing room for the
band members back in the day.)

HOT-HAMIT (HOT-HAM-mit)
translation- A replacement for Got-Damnit.

HOUNGRY (HOUN-gree) Aum *houngry*! When
we goun eat?
translation- Houngry is hungry'er than
hungry.

HOWCUM (how-cum) *Howcum* you ain't called
me till now? *or- Howcum* he gets to go,
and I don't?
translation- I don't know, WHY IS THAT?...

HUNNED (HUN-ned) I paid a *hunned* dollars
for them tires. *or-* 97, 98, 99, a *HUNNED!*
translation- One hundred

HURRUP (hur-rup) **1.** We gotta *hurrup,* we late!
2. I saw *hurrup* in the club last night actin
crazy.
translation- **1.** Hurry up... **2.** I saw HER
UP in the club...

I

I-IYT, you know aum lookin right achu, dounbe
tryin to *IGG* me!

I

I-IYT (ah-IYT) *ebncs.-* **1.** Wussup dog, you *I-iyt?*
or- Don't worry bout me, Ah be *I-iyt.*
2. *I-IYT* SIR! (*Something a brotha from the hood, in the navy, might say.*)
translation- **1.** Alright... I'll be alright. (*also see* AH-IYT) **2.** Aye aye sir. (A naval term for: I will comply.)

I-IYTDEN (ah-IYT-den) You comin by at six?
I-iytden, don't be late! *or- I-iytden*, I'll catch you later!
translation- Alright then....

I-IYTNAH (ah-IYT-nah) *I-IYTNAH!*
translation- Another word for HELLO.
(*also see* AH-IYTNAH)

IAH (EH-ya) You see, da problem *iah*, You don't know what chu doin!
or- What dat *Iah?*
translation- IS... I - S...

ICEBOX (ICE-box) Whacha got in the *icebox?*
translation- Another word for refrigerator.
(*also see* FRIGERADER)

IDNIT (ID-nit) *Idnit* bout time fadim fools tagit here?
translation- Isn't it...

IGG (igg) Ah-iyt, you know aum lookin right
   achu, dounbe tryin to *igg* me!
   translation- Ignore

IGGIN (IGG-gin) Why you *iggin* me? *or-*
   Everytime I see her, shebe *iggin* me, tryin
   to acklak I ain't there.
   translation- Ignoring

IGNANT (IGG-nant) That fool is so *ignant,* he
   don't know his ass from a hole in the
   ground!
   translation- Stupid as hell... *or,* he just don't
   know...

ILLIN (ILL-lin) While webe chillin, ya'll be *illin.*
   translation / alt. eng.- While we are here
   calmly relaxing and enjoying, you are there
   worrying, frustrated, and (might I add)
   simply NOT DOING TOO WELL.

INA-FECT (in-a-FECT) Homeboys *inafect!*
   translation- In Effect... getting something
   done...
   alt. eng.- The guys from our hometown are
   really being effective, and producing some
   positive results!

INARE (in-nare) She went back *inare* for son-in, what, I donno.
or- Chyall doin *inare?*
translation- In there... What are you all doing in there?

INERE (in-near) It's hot *inere!*
translation- In here...

INM (in-NIM) Is Mom *inm* comin by?
translation- And them...
alt. eng.- Are Mother, and the rest of the family, coming to visit?

INNA (IN-na) **1.** Ah bedare *inna* minute.
2. Where are my shoes? (*ansr.*) *Inna* closet.
translation- **1.** In a... **2.** In the...

INNA-HAYLSE (IN-na-HAIL-sss) Tyrone *inna-haylse!*
translation- In The House... (*in other words*) Tyrone is here.

INYO (IN-yo) Yo Daddy's gonna git *inyo* ass when he finds out!
translation- In your...

ISALL-GOOD (is-SALL-GOOD) You didn't show up yesterday wit my money. But chu know what? *Isall-good* cus you goun pay me right now!
translation- It's all-good... It's OK... Everything is well... Cause you WILL pay me!

ISCUZZ (ISS-cuzz) I don't understand what you're saying. *response*- *Iscuzz* you douno wadum taunmot!
translation- It's because... (*also see* SCUZZ)

ISGOUN (isss-GOUN) If you keep messin widit, *isgoun* break!
translation- It's going to... (*also see* SCONE *and* SCONNA)

ISKIDDIN (ISS-kid-den) *Iskiddin* late, can we go now?
translation- It's Getting...
(*also see* SKIDDIN)

ISSA (IS-sa) *Issa* good thang i no how 2 spell!
translation- It's a ...(good thing?)

ISSLIKE (iss-SLIKE) Well you see, *isslike*
this...
translation- It's like... someone trying to
explain something... (or get you to
BELIEVE something)

ISSN (iss-sin) Where's my jacket? (*ansr.*) *Issn*
the bakada car!
translation- IT'S IN the back seat of the car.

ISSON (is-ON) **1.** Oh, *isson* now! **2.** Where's my
lighter? (*ansr.*) *Isson* the table.
translation- **1.** It's on, (*as in-*) We gettin
ready to do somethin.
2. It's on, (*as in-*) It's on the table.

J

Those shoes are *jacdup!*

J

JACDUP (JAC-dup) Those shoes are *jacdup!*
   translation- Those shoes are ugly as hell!
   alt.eng.- Those shoes are in an incredibly
   bad state of existence!

JAC-U-UP (jack-you-up) *ebncs.*- Ah *jac-u-up* if
   you don't gimme ma money right now!
   translation- To do something punishing to a
   person, like maybe, beat um up real bad.

JALIKTA (jah-LIKE-tuh) **1.** What would *jalikta*
   do today? *or*- **2.** *Jalikta* have one of these
   Popsicle's?
   translation- (No, it's not an African name.)
   1. You like to... **2.** Would you like to...

JAMIN (JAM-min) Everytime I come to this
   club... restaurant... skating ring... beach...
   (*or whatever applies*) day be *jamin!*
   translation- Doing whatever you are doing
   in a very good way, and having a great time
   doing it!

JAMY (JAM-me) **1.** Man, that *jamy* last night
   was da bomb! **2.** Have you heard that new
   jamy by Bussa-Ryme?
   translation- **1.** Event... *as in*-club, concert,
   party, etc... **2.** song... rap... video...

JEET? (JEET) *Jeet?* No, ju? No, but am fidna!
   translation- Did you eat? No, did you? No,
   but I'm... (*see* FIDNA)

JIGGY (JIG-gy) *As I was trying on shirts in a clothing store on West 8th street in New York, the salesperson came to me and said;* If you really wanna get, ***jiggy,*** try these pants on with that shirt!
translation- To go all out... to get MORE funky... to get crazy...
(Hey, I just listen and take notes!)

JOHNSON (JOHN-son) You get your ***Johnson*** stared at when you walk in a club on ladies night.
translation- What most Black men refer to their penises as.

JONES (jones) My ***Jones*** is comin down!
OR-
JONESIN (JONES-zin) Aum ***jonessin*** for ma girl!
translation- A HABIT that you've created, and are in desperate need of.

JOINT (joint) (Not the kind u smoke) Yo chekidot, I got the new Nike ***joints!***
or- Have you heard the new by ***joint*** by Shaggy? (*also see* JAMY)
or- (maybe you remember this one) "IT'S A SPIKE LEE ***JOINT!***
translation- Dashit! (*see DASHIT*)

JU (ju) ***Ju*** do what I toldju to do?!
translation- Did you?...

K

I just *KILT* me a bigo rat!

K

KAINT (kaint) *ebncs.* If you can, you can. But if
you *kaint,* well...
translation- Do you really need one?

KEEF SWEAT (KEEF SWEAT) *translation-* The name is KEITH!
(U-no, dat singer allim girls like!)

KIKINIT (KIK-kin-nit) We just here, *kikinit* in dahood.
translation- Kicking back... Relaxing... Just here...

KIKIZAZZ (kick-kiz-ZAZZ) Amo *kikizazz* when I see him!
translation- Kick his ass... whup his butt... give him a spanking...
alt. eng.- I am going to have to punish him severely for his transgressions when he arrives.

KILLIN (KIL-lin) **1.** Ya'll was *killin* last night!
2. What's he doin inare?
(*ansr.*) *Killin* roaches.
translation- **1.** Really doing well... *alt. eng.* We went to your concert last night, and let me tell you, you were really fantastic!
2. You need a roach motel!

KILT (kil'-t) I just *kilt* me a bigo rat!
translation- Killed... (You'd know this one if you had rats.)

K-NAH (KAY-nah) *K-nah*, I tolju bout that!
   translation- A warning - OK now!

KNOCK (knock) **1.** I'll *knock* it out in the
   morning. **2.** Yo man, you *knock* that yet?
   (*ansr.*) Aw man, I been *knockin* that for 3
   months now!
   translation- **1.** To take care of a task, chore,
                     job, responsibility...
                  2. To have sex with... (it's a
                     guy thing, you'll never
                     understand)
                  3. And of course, it also means
                     to tap hard on something.
                     (Like somebody's head!)

L

(a phone call) Scuse me, I paid my bill this moanin.
When yall gone cut my *LEHCHICITY* back on?

L

LEBM (LEH-mm) *ebncs.-* 8, 9, 10, *lebm.*
translation- self explanatory

LEFF (LEFF) **1.** Bedda c'moun fo you get *leff!*
2. Turn *leff* at the next corner.
translation- **1.** Left, *as in,* you better hurry
up. **2.** Left, *as in,* don't turn right.

LEHCHIC (LEH-chic) "MAN MADE THE
LEHCHIC LIGHT...."
(It's A Man's World – James Brown)

LEHCHICITY (leh-CHIS-city) (*a phone call*)
Scuse me, I paid my bill this moanin. When
yall gone cut my *lehchicity* back on?
translation- Electricity (keep up witcho
bills!)

LEHME (leh-me) Well, *lehme* see bout that.
or- Lehme know wachu-goundo bout that
dent you put in my car.
translation- LET ME see... And LET ME
know.... soon.

LESSEET (less-SEET!) Aum hungry, *lesseet*!
translation- Let's eat.

LIKASTO (LICK-a-sto) Amma run down to the
lickasto and get me a 40.
translation- Liquor store

LODDA (LAH-duh) I won a *lodda* money at the
track yestaday. *or-* "Ah godda whole *lodda*
love fuhya baby!"
translation- A lot of...

LOOKAHEH (LOOK-ka-HEH) Now you just
lookaheh! Ah toldju amma pay you.
translation- Look here... (when?)

LOOKDID (LOOK-did) He *lookdid* funny after I
told him what you said.
translation- LOOKED! (um,um,um)

LOOKID (LOOK-kid) *Lookid* allim fools ovadar
tryin ta rap to the same woman.
translation- Look at...

LUBB (lubb) Ah *lubb* you!
*translation-*I LOVE you too.

LUFAH VANDROW (LU-fah VAN-drow) U-no ah
likes me some *Lufah Vandrow!* (*What
some of the sistas from da hood be sayin.*)
translation- LUTHER VANDROSS

M

Amma git *MABABEDADDY* to come wup yo ass!

M

MABABEDADDY (ma-bay-be-DAD-dy) *ebncs.*-
See him overdare, das *Mababedaddy!* or-
Amma git *Mababedaddy* to come wup yo
ass!
translation- My child's father.

MABAD (MA-bad) Uh-oh, *mabad!*
translation- My bad... my mistake... oops!...
alt. eng.- Sorry about that. I made a little
boo boo.

MABOYEE (ma-BOY-ee) (*Talking to the back
stage security guard*) *Maboyee* got my back
stage passes, he inare somewhere! *or*- Das
MABOYEE!
translation- Your real good friend...
(supposedly)

MABROTHA (MA-bra-tha) Wussup *mabrotha?*
translation- One of the ways we speak to, or
refer to, one another as, in a peaceful way.

MACK (mack) Check homie tryin ta *mack* on my
sister.
translation- To rap to... hit on... talk to..
impress... try to get over on...

MACK-DADDY (MACK-dad-dy) *translation-* Someone who tries to rap to... hit on... talk to... impress, many women for the sake of getting over, getting money, or whatever he can get, and has been doing it for a long time.

MAD-COOL (MAD-cool) I met the brotha yesterday, he was ***mad-cool.*** *translation-* I guess it means he was very, very cool.

MADDAFACT (MAD-duh-FACT) ***Maddafact,*** amo get me wonnym cheese samiches rat now! *translation- alt. eng.-* AS A MATTER OF FACT, I am a bit famished. I think I will partake in one or two of your delightful cheese hors d'oeuvres before dinner.

MAHNIGGAH (mah-NIG-gah) **1.** "You ***mahniggah*** if you don't git no biggah" *or-* **2.** Das ***mahniggah*** over dar! *translation-* **1.** A term of endearment expressed by two friends of African-American decent. **2.** What a proud African-American woman might say about her man.

MAMA-JAMA (MAM-ma-JAM-ma) "SHE'S A BAD *MAMA-JAMA"*
translation- She's a great woman! (She also has a song about her!)

MAMOMMA (ma-MOM-ma) Amma tale *mamomma* on you! *or-* Where *mamomma* at? *or-* I wish ma *mamomma* hurry up!
translation- My Mother

MEMBER? (MEM-ber) *Member* when we went to Grandma's house, and you was messin wit dem ducks? *Member?*
translation- Remember? (That's why you got dem duck bites on yo butt now!)

MENZIZ (MEN-ziz) All *menziz* is lazy! (*Something I heard a very intelligent Black woman, who says she's a schoolteacher, say.*)
translation- More than one men. (smirk)

MESSIKINS (MESS-si-kins) Ama go down to TJ and party wit the *Messikins!*
translation- Mexicans (We love yall. It's just that some of us can't pronounce the word MEXI.)

MESSIN (MESS-sin) Man, you bedda stop
   messin wit that stuff. *or-* Y-U-B *messin*
   around? *or-* Now you *messin* wit the
   wrong folks!
   translation- Tinkering with... bothering... *or*
   doing something you ain't suppose to be
   doing!

MINEZIZ (MINE-ziz) Is everyone's champaign
   glass ok? (*ansr.*) *Mineziz!*
   translation- Mine is... (Something I heard a
   very intelligent Black man say.)

MITCHMATCH (MITCH-match) You musta
   dressed in the dark, cuz you have
   mitchmatch sox on.
   translation- MIS-match...

MO (moe) I made *mo* money this year than last
   year.
   translation- More

MOANIN (MOAN-nin) **1.** "Topada *moanin* to
   ya!" *or-* Ah see ya'll inna *moanin.* **2.** She
   inare *moanin* cause her bird died
   yesterday.
   translation- **1.** Morning **2.** Moaning

MOBEDDA (mo-BED-da) I think this one is
mobedda than that one. *or-*
Have you seen that movie *"Mobedda*
Blues"?

MOBETTA (mo-BET-ta) *same as* MOBEDDA
(but with T's)
translation- More Better... (Hey, it's an
Ebonic thang.)

MOLDED (MOE-did) Don't get *molded* if she
don't call you back. *or-* Lavonda got *molded*
when Sandranika came in with the same
dress on lookin better than her's!
translation- The attitude you get when you
get dissed and embarrassed at the same
time. (*see* DISS)

MONEY (mon-ney) Wussup *money!?*
translation- The way people speak to you
when they think you have money.

MONKEY-ASS (MON-kee-azz) You bedda bring
yo *monkey-ass* back ova here!
translation- What you get called when you
act like fool.

MOUF (mouf) Hush yo *mouf!* *or-* You bedda
watch yo *mouf!* *or-* Put that back inyo
mouf and stop being silly! (*Things your
mother would say*)
translation- Mouth...

MOUNBAK (moun-BAK) (*A down south country
thang*) *Mounbak* nah, ya hear?!
translation- COME ON BACK...

MUDEAR (muh-DEAR) *southern ebncs.-* *Mudear*
takes us to church every Sunday.
translation- Grandmother...

MUGG (mugg) Seedat brotha playin drums
overdar? He's a bad *mugg!* *or-* I drove
that new Porsche yesterday, issa *mugg!*
translation- "MUGG" is short for "Mutha,"
which is short for "Mother," which is short
for "Mother F___!" (*also see* MUHFUH)

MUHFUH (muh-fuh) Look *muhfuh,* don't be
messin around! *or-* She's fine as a
muhfuh!
translation- Like an exclamation point...
and another way of saying "Motha Fuhka!"
(*see* MUGG)

MUNF (munf) What *munf* were you born in?
translation- Month...

MUSTA (MUS-ta) I *musta* got here too early,
cuz dinner ain't ready yet.
translation- You MUST HAVE come early
so you can COOK it.

N

Cave a **NACKIN** please?

N

NAAH (naaanh) *ebncs.*- You wanna go wit us?
(*ansr.*) **Naah.**
translation- No.
alt. eng.- No, I don't care to participate at
this time. Maybe another time.

NACKIN (NAA-kin) Cave a *nackin* please?
alt. eng.- May I have a NAPKIN, PLEASE?
translation- Napkin... paper, or cloth to
wipe your face with at the table...

NAHMEAN? (nah-MEAN)
translation- Know what I mean?

NAHUMSAYN? (nah-um-SAY-IN)
translation- Know what I'm saying?
(*also see* NOUMSAYN)

NAN (naan) You ain't got *nan* bidda sense!
translation- No sense... none...
(*also see* AHN)

NATCHEL (NAT-chel) Boy, waounchu go fix dat
natchel!
translation- Natural... Afro... (U know, that
hair style we used to wear in the '60s and
'70s, with the comb that has the fist on it
stickin out, and grownups would constantly
be telling us to go "fix it" because it would
be leaning to one side or another.)

NAYBAHOOD (NAY-ba-hood) I'm readin "The Nu *Naybahood* Funetic Ebonic Dictionary." *or-* I live inna nice **naybahood!** *translation-* It's the way we say "Neighborhood."

NEHBMINE (NEHB-mine) Didju have something you wanted to tell me? (*ansr.*) Yes I did but, ***NEHBMINE.*** *translation-* Never... mind... (The way WE say it!)

NIGGAH-PLEEZ! (NIG-ga-PLEEZ) *Niggah-pleez!* *translation-* A term of endearment only to be used by Black People. Also a response used when one of US does, or says something silly, or stupid. (Still only to be used by Black People!)

NOMO (no-moe) Ah-ounwant **nomo** dat rice! *translation-* No more... (*also see* AH-OUNWANT)

NONNA (NON-na) I don't want **nonna** that. *or-* You won't see ***NONNA*** them fools til its time to get paid! *translation-* None of...

NONYA (NON-ya) Now, you know, dat ain't *nonya* business!
translation- None of your...

NOTCHETT (knot-CHYETT) Is dinner ready? *(ansr.)* ***NOTCHETT!***
translation- Not yet...

NOTCHO (NOT-cho) That's *notcho* cheese!
translation- Not your...

NOUMSAYN (noum-SAY-in) *same as* NAHUMSAYN *but with one less syllable.*
translation- Know what I'm saying?
(see NAHUMSAYN)

N'SHIT (n-shit) Everytime we go to Grandma's house, webe eatin our asses off *n'shit!* *or-* My brother keeps a lot of cars in his driveway *n'shit.*
translation- And Shit... This is one that you can use after almost anything you say. It means that there are more things you could say about the subject, but instead you say- N'SHIT, which means- And other things... Some other stuff that I don't have to mention... You know what I'm sayin... etc. etc...

NUDAT (nu-DAT) *At the airport baggage claim, you pick up the wrong bag and someone says to you-* "Excuse me, our bags must look alike, because you just picked up MY bag." *and you reply-* "Oh... I **nudat!**" *As you embarrassedly put it back.*
translation- Knew that... (sure you did)

NUFFIN (NUF-fin) Whatchu wount? (*ansr.*) **Nuffin.**
translation- Another way of saying NOTHING. (*same as* NAU-IN)
(Hey! I ain't makin this up. I just listen to what we say and take notes!)

NUFSA-NUF (NUF-sa-NUF) C'moun nah, **nufsa-nuf!**
translation- Enough is enough...

NUH-N (NUH-in) Whachu doin? (*ansr.*) **Nuh-n.**
or- You ain't said **nuh-n** to me about it!
translation- Nothing... You aren't doing anything...
alt. eng.- You haven't mentioned anything to me concerning this matter.

NUH-UNH (nuh-UNH) *Nuh-UNH,* don't do dat!
  or- (NUH-unh) Did you do that? *(ansr.)*
  NUH-unh.
  translation- I think this is a combination of
  NO and UNH-UNH (*see* UNH-UNH)

O

O.G. (Original Gangsta)

O

O-DAH (O-dah) *ebncs.-* How *o-dah* you?
translation- Same as O-LAH, but not
pronounced as lazy. (*see* O-LAH)

ODDA (AH-da) Get *odda* ma face! *or-* Get that
thing *odda* your mouf!
translation- Out of... (*also see* OUMA)

ODDADA (AH-da-da) Michael. Go see if you can
back the car *oddada* garage.
translation- Out of the... (without hitting
anything!)

ODDAVIT (AH-da-vit) **1.** See dat bus ovadare?
My daddy gets up every mornin, and drives
the hell *oddavit!* *or-* **2.** I went to see ma
girl last night, but it must be that timemuda month, cause she was *oddavit!*
translation- **1.** He drives the heck out of it.
2. OUT-OF-IT... *as in-* Not feeling too well.

OFFDA (OFF-da) Gitcho feet *offda* couch! *or-*
That party was *offda* hook last night!
translation- **1.** Off Of The couch...
Especially with your shoes on. **2.** Off The
hook... *meaning* - Live, wild, exciting...

OFFYA (OFF-ya) Boy, what else they want, the
shirt *offya* back!
translation- same as OFFYO

OFFYO (OFF-yo) If you get *offyo* big lazy butt,
you might get somethin done roun here!
translation- Off of your...

OFRA WIMFREE (O-fra WIM-free) I heard *Ofra Wimfree* say she don't want nomo
hamburgers.
translation- OPRAH WINFREY

OFVUM (OF-vum) You know them illegal aliens
we was taunmot? I saw six *ofvum* in the
welfare line.
translation- Of them... (And what were
YOU doin there?)

O.G. (oh-gee) Original Gangsta
translation- The older gangsters... The ones that have been doing it longer then the rest. (Or so, they say) (*see* GANGSTA)

OH-SNAPP (OH-SNAPP) *Oh-snapp!*
translation- Like saying- Oh man!... Oh wow!... Oh shit!...

O-LAH (O-lah) How *o-lah* you? (*ansr.*) O-dah nuff to know diss ain't da way we posta be talkin!
translation- Old are... How OLD ARE you? (And, if das da way u talk, DAS DA way u talk. Just KNOW the difference!)

ONLYEST (OUN-lee-ist) That's the *onlyest* pair of dress shoes I got.
translation- Only... that means 1...

OUMA (OUT-ma) Git that thing *ouma* face!
translation- Out of my...

OUTCHA (OUT-cha) *same as* OUTCHO

OUTCHO (OUT-cho) You must be *outcho* mind!
or- Git dat booger *outcho* nose!
translation- Out of your....

OUTY (OU-ty) I'm *outy* 5000!
translation- A car made by Audi... *and-*
another way of saying "I'm outta here."

OVA (OH-vah) Say baby, as far as me 'n you are
concerned, its *OVA!* *or-*
Wounchu turn *ova* so you can stop snorin.
translation- **1.** Over... done... kaput... we
thu! **2.** Turn OVER.

OVADARE (o-va-DARE) You lookin for yo shoes?
They *ovadare.*
translation- Keep up with your shoes!

OWVUZ (OW-vus) *country ebncs.-* **1.** Dis one's
yourn, dat one's *owvuz.*
2. *Owvus* doin ah-iyt fo you got here.
translation- **1.** Ours... ours... That's yours,
this is OURS! **2.** I WAS...

P

PAYEESS!!

P

PACIFIC (pa-CIF-fic) *ebncs.*- When you talk to those people, you gotta be *pacific.*
translation- Ssspecific

PADUCER (pa-DUSE-cer) So, what chu do for a livin? *(ansr.)* Amma record *paducer.* Ah paduce all kinda tapes, and rappers.
or- (A beautiful young vocalist says, hopefully) My paducer said we was gonna make allkina money, soonaz he get me in his studio!
translation- PROducer huh? Studio huh? (How many times have you heard THAT one?)

PATICALLY (pa-TIC-ca-lee) *Patically* speakin, Ah don't want nonna dem fools comin roun here tryin to see ma dawda. And am talkin *patically* bout that big ugly, large foehead havin fool, wit that raggedy, smog paducin, loud speaker, no paint havin, wanna be a cadalac, need to be booted, thang he calls a car! (Something a protective father might say.)
translation- PARTICULARLY

PAYEESS (PAY-eeesss) What a rap group might say at the end of a performance while holding up two fingers- *PAYEESS!* *translation*- PEACE!

PEACE-OUT (pee-SOUT) Peace-out! *translation*- Peace, I'm outta here!... *alt. eng.*- Take care, see you later.

PEOPLES (PEE-puls) I love my *peoples!* *translation*- More than one people.

PHATT (FATT) That new Erica Badou record is kinda *phatt*, yo? *translation*- Fat... Seriously badd... *meaning,* very good (for you laymen)

PIMP-SLAP (PIMP-slap) *translation*- A *PIMP SLAP* is a slap that is done with force and vigor, in public, for the purpose of embarrassing you, and having you remember the transgressions you have committed for receiving it. (In other words, it's when you slap the "holy shit" out of somebody!)

PISA (PEE-sa) Cave a *pisa* cake? *or*- Waounchu breakmeoff a *pisa* dat. *translation*- Piece of...

You keep talkin to me like that,
and I WILL *PIMP-SLAP* you!

PISSED (pissed) Man, she was *pissed* when I didn't show up, but I cooled her out later! (Yeah right)
translation- Mad... very angry...

PISSDOFF (piss-DOFF) See, I didn't wanna tell you, now you're *pissdoff!*
translation- More mad... very very angry...

PISSMIOFF (piss-me-OFF) I know you don't wanna *pissmioff* again!
translation- Make ME mad... make ME angry, again.

PLADUHDAT (PLAY-duh-dat) The first thing amo do when I get there, is git me a *pladuhdat* food!
translation- Plate Of That...

PLAY (play) Why you tryina *play* me? *or-* Either you wake up, or you get *played!*
translation- Run a game on... Take advantage of... embarrass... Make a fool of... lead on... play with...

PLAYA (PLAY-ya) Wussup *playa*
translation- Someone (man or woman) who thinks they have their game tight with a variety of sex partners. Or they try to make it LOOK that way!

PO (POE) When we were kids growing up, we wasn't broke, we was *po!*
translation- Poor, is what poor people are. PO, is what poor'er than poor people are! In fact, Po is so poor, it can only afford 2 letters. (ba-dum bum)

POSTA (POS-sta) We *posta* start at 8.
translation- Suppose to... (*also see* SPOSE-T)

POSTABE (POST-ta-be) Who you *postabe?* or- Why ya'll makin all that noise when you *postabe* sleep?! Something your momma, daddy, or baby sitter might say.)
translation- Supposed to be...

PRECIATE (PRE-she-ate) Ahount *preciate* chu taunmot ma momma!
translation- Appreciate...
alt. eng.- I think your speaking disparagingly about my dear mother is in very poor taste.

PROPS (props) You godda give homie his *props* for allat work he been doin!
translation- Proper dues... Credit he deserves... Pay Him!

PUDIT (PU-dit) When you finish with your dirty
plate, *pudit* in the sink.
translation- Put it.

PUDUM (PUH-dum) See those dirty clothes over
there? *Pudum* in the hamper. *or- Pudum*
back where you got them from!
translation- Put them.

PUTTA (PUT-ta) *a down south ebonic thang cuz
my daddy usta say this one-* See that cup
over there? *Putta* in the sink.
translation- I guess it means Put It... *or-*
Put the...

R

My car might be *ragaly,* but it runs better than yours!

R

RADALAK (RAD-da-LAK) *ebncs.* You still drivin that *radalak!*
translation- Raggedy-ass Cadillac

RAGALY (RAG-ga-lee) My car might be *ragaly,* but it runs better than yours!
translation- Raggedy

RECONIZE (REK-con-nize) You betta *reconize!*
   translation- Recognize... to take notice of,
   and give respect to, certain individuals and
   situations around you.

RECTUM (REC-tum) Since we been married, I
   bought two cars, and she *rectum* boff!
   translation- Wrecked them... She wrecked
   both of them... Keep her butt out of the
   driver's seat!

REKASTO (REK-ka-sto) Amma go down to the
   rekasto and pick up that new Janet
   Jackson c.d.
   translation- Record Store.

REPAZENT (rep-pa-ZENT) Whether you from the
   East side, or the West side, you gotta
   repazent!
   translation- (*The word is*) re-PRE-sent

RESTADA (RES-ta-da) Ah got the *restada* day
   off. *or-* You ain't gowin nowhere until I get
   da *restada* money you owe me!
   translation- Rest of the....

RETTA (REH-ta) Aum about *retta* get up... eat... get dressed... get inna car... make this run... get wit ma Girl... Get bizzy...
translation- Ready to...

RET-TGO (ret-ta-GO) Yo, this party's wack. Aum *ret-tgo!*
translation- Ready to go... (*see* WACK)

RIYIBS (RI-yibs) *southern ebncs.-* Now, you know Ah GOTSTA git me soma dem BBQ *riyibs* while Aum there!
translation- Now, you know they must be some serious RIBS to have two syllables.

ROLL (roll) Ambouta *roll. or-* Let's *roll.*
translation- Go... leave... "Get odda dodge"... seeya...

ROLLIN (ROLL-lin) Aw, we *rollin* now!
translation- When, whatever it is we're doin, we're doin it good. We're feeling the flow.

ROUNA (ROUN-na) Aum just goin *rouna* block, Ah be back. *or-* Make sure you clean *rouna* tub after you take your bath!
translation- Around the...

127

ROUNBOUT (roun-bout) Ah be done *rounbout* seb'n.
translation- Around about...almost...just before...or just after...don't hold me to it.

RYCHIR (rye-CHEER) *southern ebncs.-* Ah be *rychir,* waiting on you to get through.
translation- Right here (of course)...

S

Yo man, all I did was take her to the mall, bought her a gold chain, and a pair of Nikes, now she's *SPRUNG!*

S

SADERNA (SAD-dern-na) *Saderna* is a proper way of saying SADNUH. (*see* SADNUH)

SADNUH (SAD-nuh) That food was *sadnuh* mugg!
translation- Sadder than a... very bad... not good at all...
alt. eng.- The meal we had last night was distasteful, and very disappointing.

SAH-EEE (sah-EEEE) WEST-*sah-EEEE!* or-
EAST- *sah-EEEE!* or even- SOUTH-*sah-EEEE!*
translation- Side- *as in*- West Side, East Side, South Side... A very proud way of proclaiming the proximity from which you hail. (But, I've yet to hear anyone say-
"NORTH-sah-EEEED!")

SALL-GOOD (SALL-good) *same as* ISALL-GOOD without the ISSS.
(*see* ISALL-GOOD)

SAMEDIFFRENCE (SAME-DIF-rence) *Everyone uses this one.*
translation- Now this one is crazy because it is two opposing terms: SAME and DIFFERENCE. Even though we know what we mean, I don't think we know what we're saying. I think I've figured it out. It's actually two sentences:
sent.- **1.** It's the SAME thing!
sent.- **2.** What's the DIFFERENCE?

SAMICH (SAM-mich) Ama go home and make me a tuna ***samich.***
translation- SAND-WICH!

SAPPNIN (SAPP-nin) *As I was walking down the street in Birmingham, Alabama, Nov. '97, I passed a brotha on the street who spoke to me saying - **"Sappnin** man?!"* *(Yeah! Brothas still speak to one another on the street down there!)*
translation- It's "Old School, " but it still works. Its short for "What's Happening?" (*see* WASSAPENIN)

SAR-IYT (sah-iyt) What did you think of the concert last night? (*ansr.*) ***Sar-iyt.***
translation- It was alright... *or-* It's alright... it was just ok... no big deal...

SCAREDA-U (SCARE-duh-U) Aum *Scareda-U!*
translation- A response to a job well done.
I'm scared of you.

SCONE (sss-CONE) *Scone* rain.
translation- same as SCONNA

SCONNA (sss-CONNA) *Sconna* be hot today.
translation- It's gonna... *or-* It's going to...
(*also see* ISGOUN)

SCOUNBE (SCOUN-be) *Scounbe* nice when we
finish it.
translation- Yes! It IS GOING TO BE nice
when we finish it!

SCREET (skreet) *southern ebncs.-* You know dat
girl wit the long braids? She lives right
downa *screet!*
translation- S-T-R-E-E-T

SCREMP (sss-KREMP) *southern ebncs.-* I'll have a
scremp salad.
translation- Shrimp (you fool!)

SCRIMINATE (SCRIM-min-NATE) Tall, short,
fat, skinny, dark, light, fine, ugly, ah-ount
scriminate, ah likes allkina womens. *or-*
Daybe *scriminate'n* against us cuz we
from dahood!
translation- DIS-criminate..

SCUSE (scuse) *Scuse* me. *or even better-* WELL, *SCUSE* DA HELL ODDA ME!
translation- Excuse... (What else could it be?)

SCUZZ (sscuzz) *Mama comes home mad from work and asked lil' Johnny-* Howcome you didn't do dem dishes like I toldju to?! *(ansr.) Scuzz,* when I was comin in to do um, Mikey called me and toll me that a monster was chasin his little sister, so we had to go save her!
translation- IT'S BECAUSE of that ridiculous answer, I'm wuppin yo butt! *(also see* ISCUZZ)

SEB'N (SEB-'n) Ama call you roun *seb'n!* *or-* 4, 5, 6, *seb'n.*
translation- **7**

SEEDAT (see-DAT) I wanna *seedat* movie when it comes out. *or-* You *seedat?*
or- Ah bleedat when I *seedat!*
translation- See that...

SEENT (seent) I *seent* him yesterday.
translation- I SAW him yesterday.

SEEUMSAYN (SEE-um-SAY-in) *Seeumsayn?*
translation- See what I'm saying?...

SEEYA (SEE-ya) **1.** *"Seeya,* wouldn't wanna be ya!" *or just plain ole-* **2.** *SEEYA! translation-* **1.** Something to say to a person who is not in good standing, that you would like to have leave. **2.** To say goodbye (in a nice way)... or to say "Get the Hell outta My face!"

SHEEYID (SHEE-id) *Sheeyid!* You know am bad! *or-* You think She's gonna meet chu at the club tonight? *(ansr.) Sheeyid!* Ah-ono. *translation-* A way of using the word Shit as an exclamation point.

SHNUFBUSTED (shon-NUF-bus-ted) When she came home and saw what was happenin, he was *shnufbusted! translation-* Sure enough busted... When you got caught, or found out....

SHOIAH (show-EEYA) You mean, he's back with that same ole crazy woman? *(ansr.) Shoiah! translation-* Sure is...

SHOLID (show-LID) And he moved that crazy ass woman back into his house? *(ansr.) Sholid! translation-* Sure did...

SHOLIZ (show-LIZ) Is that crazy ass women
   still fine? (*ansr.*) ***Sholiz!***
   translation- Sure is... (That's why he got
   back with her and moved her back in his
   house.)

SHONUFF (show-NUFF) *down south ebncs.-* Did
   you git enough to eat? (*ansr.*) ***Shonuff!***
   translation- Sure enough... *or-* Definitely!

SHO-URITE (SHOW-u-rite) ***Sho-urite!***
   translation- Sure, you're right!... *or-* Yes,
   you're telling the truth!... *or-* Preach
   Brotha! (*also see-* SHOYURAH)

SHOUT-OUT (stout-out) I wanna give a ***shout-
   out*** to my homies in cell block C!
   translation- To say Hello...

SHOYURAH (SHO-u-rah) ***Shoyurah!***
   translation- Sure, you're right (*also see-*
   SHO-URITE)

SHUDDA (SHUD-da) Ya ***shudda*** known bedda.
   translation- Should have...

SHUDNA (SHUD-na) You ***shudna*** lied aboucho
   age on your driver's license.
   translation- Shouldn't have...

SIBLE-RITES (sih-bull-rites) Yall can't fire me, I
know my *sible-rites!*
translation- (as if you needed one) Civil
Rights... Your right to know at least how to
SAY it.

SICHER (sit-CHEER) *down south ebncs.-* C'moun
in and *sichir.*
translation- Sit here...

SISTA (SIS-sta) (not sis-TER) That's a beautiful
sista over there.
translation- One of the things we refer to
Black Women as.

SITCHIATION (sit-chi-A-shon) Don't worry, Ah
got the *sitchiation* under control. (yeah,
right)
translation- SITUATION

SKANK (SKANK) *translation-* One of the things
we refer to nasty, lyin, stealin, dope doin,
crack head, screw anybody, women as.

SKEEZA (SKEE-za) *translation-* One example is:
A woman who appears to be nice, but will
screw you, and your best friend, for your
money and whatever else she thinks you
have, sneak and go through your pockets,
lie about it, and will look good doing it!
(*also see* HOOCHIE)

SKIDDIN (SKID-in) *Skiddin* cold in here, can you turn on some heat?
translation- ITSKIDDIN *(just kidding)* It's getting...

SKILLS (skills) You godda have yo *skills* together to hang wit the big boys!
translation- Abilities... Know how... Smarts...

SKOEET (sko-EET) Aum hungry, *skoeet!*
translation- Self explanatory... (ok) Let's go eat...

SKOUNBE (SKON-be) The concert tonite *skounbe* a mugg!
translation- IT'S GOING TO BE... *(same as SCOUNBE, but with a K)*

SKRATE (ssss-KRATE) **1.** Tagit to the store, you godda go *skrate* downa screet, and turn left at the fire hydrant. **2.** You want another beer? *(ansr.)* Naw, I'm *skrate.*
translation- **1.** Straight, *as in* go straight.
2. Straight, *as in* I'm ok... I'm alright I've had enough... Aum good... Ah godda drive!

SKRADADA (SKRAY-DA-da) Dis book is *skradada* dahood!
translation- Straight out of...

SKRADOUT (skray-DOUT) Ama tell ya'll *skradout*, don't mess wit me while am eatin!
translation- Straight Out... Direct... Like it is!...

SLAMIN (SLAM-min) Damn girl! Them greens was *slamin!*
translation- Very, Very Good!
alt. eng.- My goodness! Those collard greens were delightfully delicious!

SMO (smo) Want *smo*?
translation- Do you want SOME MORE?...

SMUV (smoov) Aw girl, yo skin so *smuv.*
translation- Smooth, smooth!

SNAPPIN (SNAP-pin) *translation*- When you and a friend are jokingly exchanging pleasantries (NOT!) about each other's momma, shoes, clothes, car, house, breath, hairdo, doorag (you know, that rag that you put around your head to keep your "just done" hair in place), girlfriend, boyfriend, husband, wife, or whatever, in a not so pleasant way. (*also see* DISS)

SNOT (snot) *Snot* what you think it is.
translation- I know you thought it was
something else, but IT'S NOT.

SOMADDA? (som-MAD-da) *Somadda?* Yo dog
died or son-in?
translation- What's the matter?
(*also see* WASSUMADDA)

SOMADAT (som-ma-dat) I drove 20 miles, in the
rain, just to get *somadat* B.B.Q.!
translation- You could've gotten SOME OF
THAT, around the corner from your house.

SOONAZ (SOON-naz) I swear I'll do it, *soonaz* I
get back!
translation- Soon as... (How many times
have you heard THAT one?)

SON-IN (SON-in) (*an east coast thang*) **1.** Did ju
say *son-in?* *or-* Ah godda do *son-in*. Ah
can't just sit here and do nau-in. *or-*
Waounchu breakmeoff a lil *son-in, son-in*.
translation- Something... The opposite of
Nothing... (*see* NAU-IN)

SPENTIT (SPIN-tit) "Ah *spentit* all dis money
on dis suit, and we didn't even win da prize"
(From the '98 Gramys)
translation- SPENT... (*as in,* you wasted
your money!)

SPLAIN (splane) I don't know why he didn't
splain it the first time. *or-* How many
times do I have to *splain* myself?
cubonics- "LUCY! YOU GOT SOME
SPLAINING TO DO!"
translation- Explain... Explaining...

SPOSE-T (spose-t) Who you *spose-t* be?
or- Aum *spose-t* get paid today.
translation- Supposed to...
(*also see* POSTA)

SPRUNG (sss-PRUNG) Yo man, all I did was take
her to the mall, bought her a gold chain,
and a pair of Nikes, now she's *sprung*.
(*yeah right*)
translation- In love... head over hills... can't
do without you...

SRONG (sss-WRONG) *Srong* witchu man, yo
feet hurt?
translation- What's wrong?... *or-* What is
wrong?...

STANK (STANK) **1.** Yo breff *stank!*
2. Yomama's a *stank*-hoe! (just kidding)
translation- **1.** STANK smells worst then
STINK! **2.** STANK-hoe is a woman that
will do ANYTHING for money, to get high,
to eat, to get laid, and is NASTY in the
process.

STANNAT (stan-nat) Whatchu *stannat?*
translation- What are you STARING AT?

STISSTISSTIC (stiss-TISS-tick) *I was at a*
friend's house who has two dogs. A young
lady came in and said - "Dassa mean
dog! Ah-ounwanna get bit and become no
stisstisstic!" *I then said "excuse me?" (just*
to make sure I heard right.) She then
repeated the word "stisstisstic." *I could've*
corrected her at that point but, she seemed
so adamant about her pronunciation, I
said to myself, "what the hell, amo add it to
my book!"
translation- STA-TIS-TIC

STOLE (stole) He *stole* on him when he wasn't
lookin!
translation- Punched him... He stole a
punch...

STUDIN (STUD-in) I ain't *studin* you.
 translation- Thinking about... or studying

STUPID (STU-pid) Man, that girl was *stupid* fine!
 translation- Extremely...

SUP (SUP) *Sup!*
 translation- Short for WUSSUP.
 (*see* WUSSUP)

SUP-WITCHU (SUP-wit-chu) Yo man, *sup-witchu?*
 translation- What's up with you?... What is going on with you?... What is wrong with you?... How are you doing?... How have you been?... (*also see* WUSSUP)

SUP-WITDAT (SUP-wit-dat) *Sup-witdat?*
 translation- see WUSSUP-WITDAT

SWET-IN (SWE-in) **1.** Why you *swet-in* me man?! **2.** You *swet-in!* You been runnin or son-in?
 translation- **1.** To bother, pressure, or bug.
 2. To perspire, or sweat... to work hard...

S'WUT (s-WUT) **1.** Now dat *s'wut* am taunmot!
or- **2.** *S'wut* ah said!
translation- **1.** THAT'S WHAT I'm talking about. **2.** THAT'S WHAT I said.

SYKE (syke) Yomamma just called and said she won 9 million dollars in the lottery, and she said she bought you and her new cars, and will buy you all the clothes you want!
SYKE!!
translation- PSYCH *as in-* NOT! *as in-* I fooled you... I was just joking...

T

Scuse me, I took a hit of this joint, and now aum
TRIPPIN.

T

TADAT (ta-DAT) I can't wait to get back *tadat* party!
translation- To that

TA-DOW! (ta-DOW) *translation-* Something you might loudly say when:
  1. You want to suprise someone special with that gift certificate from your favorite 99 cent store!
  2. When you come home and show yo momma your first paycheck from your first job that she didn't think you'd ever get.
  3. When you are describing to one of your friends, the size of one of your other friend's sister's butt. *(Yall know yall doodat!) (also see* BOO-YA)

TAGIT (tuh-GIT) It's time *tagit* PAID!
translation- To Get....

TAUNMOT (TAUN-mot) Man, I saw him yestaday, but he wadnt *taunmot* nothin.
or- Now dat s'wut AUM *taunmot*!
translation- Talking about

TEDDY PENDAGRAM (TED-DY PEN-da-gram)
Girl lehme tall ya, back in the day, me, my
sister, AND mamomma threw our draws at
Teddy Pendagram during his concert!
(*Something I overheard two women in their
50s say.*)
translation- PENDAGRASS... TEDDY
PENDAGRASS!!

TEEF (TEEF) Ricky! Go brush yo *teef!*
translation- Self explanatory

TEET (teet) You wont son-in *teet*?
translation- TO EAT... Do you want
something TO EAT?

TELLER (TELL-ler) (*We ain't talkin bout no bank
teller neither*) When you see Yomama,
teller to wipe dat boogah off her face!
translation- Tell Her

TELLIM (TELL-lim) **1.** When I see yo daddy,
amo *tellim* his breff ments ain't workin!
2. Woodju please *tellim* fools to stop talkin
about each other's parents!
translation- **1.** Tell Him **2.** Tell THEM...

TELLUM (TELL-lum) *Tellum* yoself!!
translation- Tell THEM

THE-LAND (*the*-LAND) I can't wait till we get
back to *the-land*!
translation- Another term for dahood...
neighborhood...

THONDOWN (thonn-DOWN) I just left the club
where the band was playin. Boy, they was
thondown!
translation- Throwing Down...
alt. eng.- They were really playing great,
sounding good, and everyone was having a
great time!

THUDAT (THEW-dat) I went *thudat* wit him
yesterday.
translation- THROUGH THAT... When you
go through an experience with someone.

THUDOWN (thu-DOWN) You *thudown* on that!
translation- Threw down...
(*like* THONDOWN)
alt. eng.- Your performance was exceptional
and brilliant.

TIGHT (TIght) Man, dem shoes are *tight*!
translation- Nice... Those shoes are very, very nice!

TIL (TIL) I can't wait *til* you get home!
translation- Until...

TIMEMUDA (TIME-muh-duh) Daddy told me not to bug Mommy cause it was THAT *timemuda* month.
translation- Do you really need one?

TIP (tip) *old school ebncs.-* We gettin ready to *tip*.
translation- TIP... *as in* -tip toe... leave... lets go... see ya!

TOEBAK (TOE-bak) We went out and got *toebak* last night!
translation- Tore back... *meaning-* Drunk as hell!.. *or just plain ole* Inebriated. ("Inebriated" look THAT one up in Webster's)

TOEDOWN (toe-down) My sister's kids came over yesterday, and damn near *toedown* the house!
translation- Tore down... (You know how dose kids do!)

When he finally came home from the club last night, he was **TOEBAK!**

TOEJAM (TOE-jam) Hey baby, I ain't rubbin, or touchin them feet until you do son-in bout them **toejams**!
translation- Toe jam - crusty, dingy, rock looking things jammed up between your toes.

TOELER (TOE-ler) All he **toeler** was how foine she was, now she's sprung.
translation- Told Her (*see* SPRUNG)

TOELIM (TOE-lim) I *toelim* he couldn't come here wit dat weak ass line, tryin ta mack on my sister! (*see* MACK)
translation- Told Him

TOELUM (TOE-lum) Mamomma came in here and *toelum* she didn't want no foolishness between num.
translation- Told Them

TOELUS (TOE-lus) Then she *toelus* all to get the hell odda here!
translation- Told Us

TOEUMUP (TOE-um-UP) **1.** We played ball witdum yesterday and *toeumup!*
2. I bought him a pair of shoes yesterday, and he *toeumup* already!
translation- **1.** Won the game and beat them badly! **2.** Tore them up...wore them out.

TOEUP (toe-UP) Man, that car is *toeup*! Waounchu fix it, or get a new one.
translation- (*you figure it out!*)

TOLDIM (TOLL-dim) *Ah toldim* whachu said.
translation- Told him... said to him...

TOLDER (TOLL-der) He *tolder* he was all in love wit her.
translation- Told her... said to her...

TOLJU (TOL-ju) Ah *tolju* he was lyin!
   translation- Told you... said to you...

TOLME (TOLL-me) She *tolme* he was lyin too.
   translation- Told me... said to me...

TOOF (toof) My gold *toof* fell out when we was
   dancin at the club last night.
   translation- Tooth... the kind you bite with...

TRIPPIN (TRIP-pen) **1.** Y.U.B. *trippin* so hard?
   or- She *tripps* hard when ever she sees
   HIM speaking to OTHER women. **2.** Scuse
   me, I took a hit of this joint, and now aum
   trippin.
   translation- **1.** Being moody... acting crazy...
   acting abnormal... Get a life!
   2. What happens when you get high. (*Just
   Say No!*)

U

(knock, knock)   Hey! Ah gotta git inna baffroom!
U-BOUTHU?

U

U-B (you-be) *ebncs.- U-B* trippin sometimes.
  translation- Self explanatory
  (*see* TRIPPIN)

U-BOUTHU? (you-bout-THU) (*knock, knock*)
  Hey! Ah gotta git inna baffroom!
  U-bouthu? (*as you're dancin and squirmin*)
  translation- Are you about through?

U-DA-MAN (U-da-MAN) *U-DA-MAN!*
  translation- You are the Man... Something
  you say to a guy who does something
  exceptionally well.

U-DA-ONE (U-da-ONE) Aw baby, you know
  u-da-one!
  translation- You are the one... Something
  you might say to your lady to let her know
  that she's your "One and Only."

U-GO (you-GO) *U-go* boy! *or- U-go* girl!
  translation- Short for "There you go!" It's
  like a pat on the back.

U-NO (you-NO) **1.** *U-no* her? *or-* **2.** A'man, Am
gih-in tired of this, *u-no*?
translation- **1.** DO YOU KNOW her?
2. DO YOU KNOW what I'm saying?
(*see* Nahumsayin?*)*

U-ONO (YOU-oh-no) *U-ono* whachu taunmot!
translation- You don't know...
alt. eng.- You have NOT the knowledge, *or*
the details you need, to discuss this matter!

U-WOUNCHO (you-WOUN-cho) *U-wouncho*
money now, or later?
translation- Do you want your...

UHBM (UH-bum) I want three *uhbm*....to go.
translation- I would like to have three OF
THEM to go, please.

UHDIM (uh-dim) Ah got one *uhdim* big ones!
(yeah, right)
translation- Of them... (*also see* WONNYM)

UHDOSE (uh-dose) Three *uhdose* are mine!
translation- Of those...
(*also see* UHVUM *and* UHDIM)

UHRUH (uh-ruh) *ebncs. in court-* Well your Honor, *uhruh*, you see, *uhruh*, I wasn't goin as fast as the poe-lise man SAID I was goin cause, *uhruh*, all the other cars were goin, *uhruh*, way slower than mines!
translation- Do you really need one?
(*also see* BUTUH, AN-NUH-UH *and* UH-RUMM)

UHRUMM (uh-rumm) *same as* UHRUH *but with* RUM

UHTHA (UH-tha) Gimme another one, just like the *uhtha* one!
translation- Other...

UHTHAN-NAT (UH-than-NAT) I said what I had to say yesterday, *uhthan-nat,* Ah ain't got nothin else to say! *or-* The house note is paid, the car note is paid, the lights are on, the kids got food, *uhthan-nat*, Aum straight.
translation- Other than that...

UNH-UNH (UNH-unh) Did ju think you were ever gonna see this word in any dictionary? (*ansr.*) *UNH-unh.*
translation- No, neither did I!
(*also see* NUH-UNH)

UHVUM (UH-vum) *same as* UHBM

UPINERE (up-in-EAR) Its gettin hot ***upinere***!
translation- Up in here.

USABE (YOU-sa-be) He ***usabe*** one of the riches
brothas around before he started hittin that
pipe!
translation- (and this is important)
USED TO BE!

USTA (USE-ta) He ***usta*** be a crack head before
he cleaned his self up. Now he has a job, a
car, and is gettin ***usta*** the idea of having
money in his pocket!
translation- USED TO... (Which, in this
context, is also very important!)

USTA-COULD (USE-ta-could) I ***usta-could***
doodat before my brain surgery.
translation- Used to be able to...

W

Everytime I spray...dem roaches start runnin
every *WITCHAWAY!*

W

WACHOT-NA (wa-CHOT-na) *ebncs.- Wachot-na, I'm comin through! or- When one of your old-school, wanna be hip, uncles comes to your birthday party and pulls out one of his "Back Then" dance steps, he might say; Wachot-na, yall don't know bout this one!* *translation-* Watch Out Now...

WACK (wack) That was *wack*!
translation- Not happenin... wrong... not good... messed up...
alt. eng.- That was a deplorable situation!

WADATIZ (WHA-dat-iz) *Wadatiz?*
translation- What that is?... *which should be-* What is that?

WADDA (WAH-duh) We posta be drankin 8 glasses of *wadda* a day! *(spoken from the mouth of a noted nutritionist. Dr. R.M.)*
translation- WATER... 8 glasses a day...

WADELS (wa-DELSE) So, *wadels* is new?!
translation- What... else...

WADEVA (wah-DEH-va) **1.** *Wadeva* happened to that old man who lived in the house on the corner wit alla bats in the bushes on his porch? **2.** *or just plain ole-* **WADEVA!** *translation-* **1.** WHAT EVER *as in-* What happened to... Where is... Do you know anything about?... **2.** WHAT EVER *as in-* It don't matter to me!

WADUP-WITDAT (wa-DUP-wit-dat) *see* WUSSUP-WITDAT

WADIZ (WHA-diz) *Wadiz* the name of that song you be singing alla time?
translation- What is...

WADIZAT (WHA-diz-ZAT) **1.** So, *wadizat* mean, you ain't comin? *or-*
2. You know that thing you brought in here yesterday? *Wadizat*?
translation- **1.** WHAT DOES THAT mean?
2. WHAT IS THAT anyway?

WALLAMILLIN (WAL-la-mill-lin) I want a big juicy pisa dat *wallamillin*!
translation- Watermelon

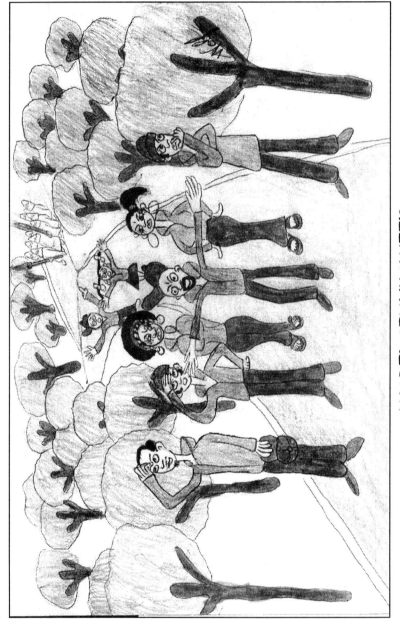

WAREDAFUHKAWEE!?

WAOUNCHU (WAH-oun-chu) *Waounchu*
shuddup!
translation- Why don't you...
(*also see* WYOUNCHU)

WAREDA (WARE-da) Scuse me, *wareda*
baffroom at?
translation- Behind the preposition; At.
(ok, sorry) Where is the...

WAREDAFUHKAWEE (WARE-da-fuh-KA-wii)
translation- This is a tribe of people who are
travelers, and sometimes wanderers, who
got their name from a chant they would
sing loud, and many times, when they were
lost. (This tribe was once discovered by Mr.
Redd Fox)

WAREYAT? (ware-yat) Wassup man, *wareyat?!*
translation- Where are you at?... A way of
asking, "how are you doing?"

WAREZZ (warezzz) *Warezz* my money?!
translation- Well, WHERE IS my money?
(Damnit!)

WASHEE (WAS-shee) *Washee* fine!? *Washee* alone!? *Washee* rich!? Or *washee* a bitch widda bad attitude?
translation- Well, WAS SHE?

WASSAMADDA? (wus-sah-MAD-da-?) *Wassamadda* witchu?
translation- WHATS THE MATTER with me? (*also see* SOMADDA)

WASSAPPENIN (wus-SAP-pen-nin) *old school ebncs.-* *Wassappenin* yall!? *or-* *Wassappenin* upinere?
translation- What's happening?... (*also see* WASSUP, SUP, and SAP·NIN)

WASSUP (wus-SUP) *Wussup* yall?!
translation- What is up...What is going on...What is happening?... Hi you guys!... Hello!... (*also see-* SUP)

WASSUP-WITDAT (wus-SUP-wit-dat) *Wussup-witdat* girl around the corner?
translation- What is going on with the beautiful lady around the corner?

WAY-N (WAY-nn) I been *way-n* out here for two
   hours!
   translation- WAIT-TING (*As in,* What took
   you so long?!)

WAYMINIT (WAY-min-nit) *Wayminit*, what
   time we posta bedare?
   translation- Wait a minute...

WE-DABIN (WE-duh-bin) *We-dabin* here a long
   time ago if the traffic wuh'int so bad! *or-*
   We-dabin there all night if they didn't
   close the bar, stop the music, and make
   everybody put their clothes back on.
   translation- We would have been... (also a
   standard excuse)

WEDA (WE-da) *Weda* People of the United
   States... *or-* Are *Weda* only ones dat talk
   like dis?
   translation- WE THE... (The first few words
   of the Preamble to the Constitution of the
   United States, the way WE say it)

WEEBE (WE-be) *Weebe* eatin our asses off roun
   Thanksgiving and Christmas!
   translation- Well, WE DO BE eatin....

WHACHAMACALLIT (WHA-cha-ma-call-lit-?)
translation- When you can't think of the name of whatever it is you're looking for. WHAT DO YOU CALL IT?

WHACHAMAJIGGUM (WHA-cha-ma-jig-gum-?)
translation- When you can't think of the name of the person you are looking for. WHATS HIS NAME?

WHACHU (WHA-chu) *Whachu* say about mamomma?
translation- Well, WHAT DID YOU say? (*also see* WHAJU)

WHACHU-GOUNDO (wha-chu-goun-do)
Whachu-goundo bout that hole in yo natural?
translation- WHAT ARE YOU GOING TO DO about your receding hairline?

WHACHU-TAUNMOT? (WHA-chu taun-mot)
Whachu-taunmot you ain't payin me my money? *or- "**WHACHU-TAUNMOT WILLIS?!**"*
translation- What (on earth) are you talking about? (Usually, this is a prelude to a butt kickin.)

WHACHU-WONT? (WHA-chu WONT) *(someone calls)* JIMMY! *(Jimmy answers)* ***Whachu-wont?!***
translation- What Do You Want?

WHACHYALL (WHA-chyall) ***Whachyall*** goundu bout dem fleas yo dog got all ova yo yard, and mines?!
translation- What are you all... *(You're on your own with the rest of this sentence.)*

WHADAH (WHA-dah) **1.** ***Whadah*** tell you to do? **2.** Das ***whadah*** said!
translation- **1.** What did I... **2.** That's WHAT I said...

WHADEE (WHA-dee) **1.** ***Whadee*** do? **2.** He was talkin, but nobody understood ***whadee*** said.
translation- **1.** WHAT DID HE do? **2.** WHAT HE said... ("Talkin loud and sayin nothin.")

WHADISOMEVA (WHA-dis-some-EH-va) *a really country ebonic way of saying-* Whatever.

WHADUM (WHA-dum) *Whadum* tryin to do is
   splain myself so you noumsayn.
   Nahumsayn? (*see* NOUMSAYN *and*
   NAHUMSAYN)
   translation- WHAT I AM...

WHAJU (wha-ju) *Whaju* do last night? *or-*
   Whaju get from the mall?
   translation- What did ju... (sorry) you...
   (*also see* WHACHU *and* WUHJU)

WHODAT (WHO-dat) *Whodat* say *whodat*
   when I say *whodat*?
   translation- Who is that?
   (*also see* WHOZDAT)

WHODIS (who-DIS) *Phone rings, man answers
   and says:* Hello?... *Whodis?*
   translation- Who is this?

WHOWAZAT (WHO-waz-ZAT) *or-* (WHO-waz-
   DAT) *Whowazat* said dey was hungry? *or-*
   Whowazdat inna bakada car witchu the
   uhtha night?
   translation- Who was that...

WHOZAT (WHO-ZAT) **1.** *Whozat* the door?
2. *Whozat* shirt belong to?
translation- **1.** Who is at... **2.** Who does
that...

WHOZDAT (whoz-DAT) *Whozdat* in da back,
bangin on da back door?
translation- Who is that?...

WHOZISDAT? (WHO-zis-DAT) *or-* (WHO-zis-
ZAT) *Whozisdat*?
translation- Whose is that?... Who does that
(item) belong to?

WIDDA (WID-da) Man, I saw Kevin yesterday
widda bigo fat woman that looked like a
man!
translation- With a... (and it probably was)

WIDDIT (WID-dit) You talkin allat mess, c'moun
widdit!
translation- Something you might say, as a
challenge, just before - a basketball game...
a fight... or a sexual encounter... *It means*
WITH IT... Bring it on!

WIGGIN (WIG-gin) Just cuz she's buggin, you can't be *wiggin!*
                              OR-
WIGGINNOUT (WIG-gin-NOUT) Ain't chyall tired of *wigginnout* about the same thing over and over?
translation- Wigging out... going crazy... having uncontrollable anger... calm down... get a life! (*same as* BUGGIN)

WINDEE (WIN-dee) *Windee* say he was goun show up with the food?
translation- When Did He...

WIT (wit) You gotta come *wit* son-in biggernat!
translation- With...

WITCHAWAY (WITCH-ah-way) Everytime I spray...dem roaches start runnin every *witchaway*!
translation- Get a roach motel!

WITCHU (wit-CHU) Aum comin *witchu*.
translation- With you

WITDAT (wit-DAT) Whachu-goundo *witdat*?
translation- With what? (oh, I'm sorry)... With That

WOEMEOUT (woe-me-OUT) Man, she *woemeout* last night!
translation- WORE ME OUT (Yeah, you probably got your butt kicked... got your feelings hurt... got embarrassed... and had a great time!)

WOEOUT (woe-OUT) Man, dem sox are *woeout*.
translation- Very tired.... wore out...

WONFAH (WON-fah) I bought *wonfah* $2.00 yesterday. *or- Wonfah* da money, two for da show!
translation- one for

WONFAHDAT (won-fah-DAT) If it *wonferdat*, I'd be livin large!
translation-. If it WASN'T FOR THAT...

WONMOGINN (won-mo-GIN) We gonhata do dis *wonmoginn*!
translation- Once more again... one more time...

WONNA (WON-na) So whachu *wonna* do?
translation- What ever you WANT TO do.

WONNADEEZ (WON-NA-deez) **1.** *Wonnadeez* days amma get me a bigo house wit nine bedrooms!
or- (won-na-DEEZ) **2.** I want *wonnaDEEZ,* *wonnaDEEZ,* and of course, *wonnaDEEZ.*
translation- (of course) ONE OF THESE...

WONNYM (won-NIM) I want *wonnym* green ones.
translation- Wonnym... (just kidding) ONE OF THEM or THOSE.

WONT (wont) Whachu-wont?
translation- WANT. But we say it like WON'T.

WOODJU (WOOD-ju) *Woodju* please stop makin that noise!
translation- Would you...

WOOGIE (WOO-gie) What you would do to a baby, (or anybody) when you put your lips on their stomach and blow, getting that biggo fart sound. (*see* FART)

171

WORUMOUT (wor-um-MOUT) We went to the
  Lakers game last night, they *worumout*!
  translation- Self explanatory (except for
  who wore out who?)

WUH'DNA (WUD-n-na) *Wuh'dna* hell you do
  wit my hammer? *or-Wuh'dna* world is
  that?!
  translation- What in the...

WUH'DNT (WUD-int) If it *wuh'dnt* fuh you, I'd
  be rich by now!
  translation- Wasn't... was not...

WUHJU (WUH-ju) *Wuhju* pay fadim shoes?
  translation- What did you... (*or better yet*)
  How much?

WUNMO (won- MO) All I need is *wunmo* and am
  good! *or-* Baby please, just *wunmo*?
  translation- Baby please!

WURZDUH (WURS-duh) *Wurzduh* ketchup?
  translation- Well, where is it?... *or-* Where
  is the.....

WUSSHER (WUSH-sher) *Wussher* name?
  (*also the same as* WUSSHO)

WUSSHO (WUSH-sho) *Wussho* sign?
  translation- What's your... (*see* WUSSHER)

"*WUSSONEVA* I PLAY, IT GOSTA BE FUNKY"

WUSSONEVA (WUS-son-EV-va)
  (Make It Funky... J.B.)
  translation- I guess what he's trying to say
  is- WHATEVER I play...
  (You know J.B. will Make It Funky)

WUZGONNA (wuz-GUN-na) I *wuzgonna* do it
yesterday, but...
translation- This is a term (or excuse) that
most people use that is both PAST, (*WAS*)
and FUTURE, (*GONNA*) and has nothing
to do with Now! Which is when you should
have DONE what you said you was gonna
DO in the first place!

WUZWIT (wuz-wit) **1.** *Wuzwit* dat? *or- Wuzwit*
dem funny lookin shoes? *or- Wuzwit* dem
fools overdar? **2.** Who was Debbie wit last
night? (*ansr.*) She *wuzwit* that crazy ass
Hakim!
translation- **1.** What's with... **2.** Was with...

WUZZAT (wuz-ZAT) *Wuzzat* a green one, or a
blue one?
translation- Was that...

WYDE (WHY-dee) *Wyde* say what he said when
he didn't mean it?
translation- WHY DID HE say that....

WYDEHBE (WY-deh-bee) *Wydehbe* trippin so
hard
translation- WHY ARE THEY acting that
way? *or-* Why DO they...

174

WYDIDODAT (WHY-dee-do-DAT) So, *wydidodat* when you told him not to? *translation*- Why DID he do that? You tell me!

WYHEBE (WY-he-be) *Wyhebe* messin wit dat stuff? *translation / alt. eng.*- Why is he involving himself with those illicit substances?

WYOUNCHU (WHY-oun-chu) Yo! *Wyounchu* say whachu gotta say, and then, get the hell otta here! *translation*- So, WHY DON'T YOU? (*also see* WAOUNCHU)

WYSHEBE (WY-she-be) *Wyshebe* flirtin wit everybody? *translation*- Why does she?... (cause she's a tease!)

WYZDAT (WYZ-dat) Everytime I tell you to do one thing, you do zackly the opposite. *Wyzdat*? *translation*- Why is it that....

y

YOMAMA!

y

Y-U-B (WHY-YOU-BE) *ebncs.-* ***Y-U-B*** messin
wit me alla time?!
translation- Very self-explanatory!

YALL (yall) Ha *yall* doin?!
translation- Do YOU ALL really need one?

YALL'S (yalls) Dares *yall's* bus right dare!
translation- You all's bus... All *yall's* bus...
You guyses bus... All of your's bus...
The bus is here, you guys!

YALLDONE (YALL-done) **1.** *Yalldone* came in
here, cleaned the room, and then toe-it back
up in the same 15 minutes! *or-*
Yalldone didit now!
2. *Yalldone?*
translation- **1.** You All Have Done... **2.** Are
You All Done?

YALL'LONO (YALL-lone-no) *Yall'lono*
whachyall doin!
translation- YOU ALL DON'T KNOW what
you all are doing. (*also see* WHACYHALL)

YAMO (YA-mo) *"YAMO BE THERE!"* or- *Yamo* do it tomorrow.
translation- Yeah, amo be there... *or-* Yes, I'm going to...

YESTIDEH (YES-teh-deh) You lookin fuh Gene? I saw him *yestideh* goin down the screet.
translation- Yesterday

YEHSO (YEH-so) *Yehso,* what we goundu next?
translation- Yes, so... This usually means that you agree, and don't want to hear any long explanation, and are ready to move on to something else.

YIONYOWN (Yion-Yown) Well yall, I hate to tell you but, *Yionyown!*
translation- This is one of the favorite things Stevie Wonder's road manager likes to say on the last day of a tour: "You're On You're Own!"
or to be exact- "It's Yo Yo Day!"
(Yeah Charlie, you big...)

YO (yo) **1.** *Yo,* wussup?! **2.** *Yo* breff stanks!
translation- **1.** Another way of saying; Hey you... hi... excuse me... pssst... can't you see I'm tryin to get your attention?! **2.** Your

YOMAMA (yo-MOM-ma) *YOMAMA!*
>*translation-* This is a term used by
>FRIENDS (unless you want to get your ass
>kicked) as a response, or rebuttal, to a
>statement made in jest (hopefully) from one
>to another, about something (or in this case,
>someone) personal.

YOSELF (yo-self) "YOU BEDDA CHECK
>*YOSELF* B4 U BREAK *YOSELF"*
>*translation-* YOUR SELF!

YOURN (yourn) *this is some country ebncs.-* This
>one is mine. That one is *yourn.*
>*translation-* I think he's trying to say -
>YOUR'S.

YOUZA (YOU-za) *Youza* lie! *or- Youza* badd
>muhfuh!
>*translation-* You are a... ("badd muhfuh"
>*meaning-* A great guy!)

YUDON (YOU-don) *Yudon* pissed me off now!
>*translation-* You have done...
>*alt. eng.-* You have made me very angry!

Z

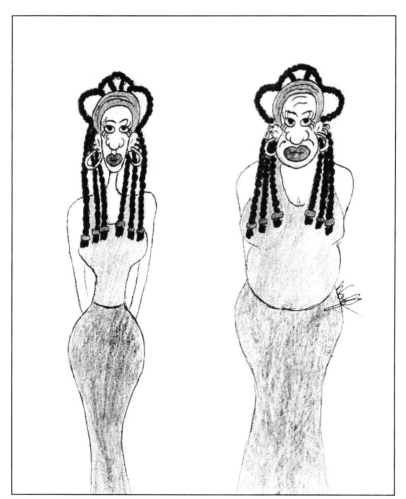

She look *ZACLAK* her momma!

Z

ZACLAK (ZAK-lak) *ebncs.-* She look *zaclak* her momma!
translation- Exactly like...

ZAKLY (ZAK-ly) Why woodju come in here, and do *zakly* the opposite of whachu did yesterday?
translation- EXACTLY what do you mean?

ZAT (zat) *Zat* all you wanted to say? *or- Zat* the way it is?
translation- Is that...

ZATCHU? (zat-CHU) G'dog, *zatchu*?
translation- G, dog, (the name of the person whom you are inquiring about) IS THAT YOU?

ZATRITE (ZAT-rite) *Zatrite*? We at the enda dis book?
translation- IS THAT RIGHT? Well yes, that is right, and it's a good thing too, cuz after listening to "US" talk, say things, and express ourselves, I was hearing new stuff everyday, I thought I'd NEVA get thu! But we thu, (for now) and we hope you learned something!

ACKNOWLEDGMENTS

I thank GOD for blessing me with a wonderful life, and a wonderful opportunity to share this life with some very special people; Maria, Franchesca, Gyasi Salif, Abuela Carmen Martinez, Darryl Jr. "Wolf" (mi familia). Arthur Jackson Jr. (Pops), Eugenia Jackson (Moms, who is sitting proudly with the angels, watching over us!), Art III, Gene, Akiba, Fran, and Denise (Brothers and sisters who be keeping each other's back). Much love to yall!

Now, u know how WE do it. Whenever you pickup a book, CD, or wadeva, written by one of US, webe thankin everybody from our mommas to the milkman! Webe thankin uncles and cousins we ain't seen in years! Webe thankin friends who ain't had nuh-in to do with the project, but might get mad if they don't see their name, especially if they see someone else's name they know! But, "on the real," without the many friends, family, and associates who have showered me with love, support, and "positive vibes" all my life, and just plain ole be'n their self, this work would not have been done. (At least by me.) So, without any further ado- and remember, this is just to name a FEW! I'd like to thank------- Benny and Lovey Jackson, Jacquelyn Levi, Sean and Tamara Jackson, Gloria Vincent, JoAnn Fountan, Uncle Leslie, Aunt Nellie (Lutcher), Aunt Florida, Aunt Margie, Kamauu Daaood, Sekou Bunch, Rayford Griffin, Dianne Reeves, Chris Severin, Herlin Riley, David Torkanowsky, Conan Reynolds, Ricky Sabastian, Bill and Yvette Summers, Angel Figueroa, Alisa Owens, Jonathan Butler, Bernard Davis "mosky," Mindy Abair, Artie Reynolds, E. Kevin Jones, Big Black, Skip Burney, Quentin Dennard, Billy Mitchell, John Bolivar, Sufia DeSilva, Marina Bambino, Chann Berry, Terri Lyne Carrington, George Duke, Ndugu, Stevie Wonder, Nate Watts, Gerry Brown, Herman Jackson, Rick Zuniga, Morris O'Conner, Rodney Franklin, Doctor Gibbs, Doc Powell and Charlene, Keb Mo, Johnny Jones, Gimi Taylor,

Keith and Fay Jones, Debra Laws, Ronnie Laws, Eric McKain, Francis Awe, Greg Walker, Harold Lott, Joe Addington, Joan Kelly and Russell Taylor, John Otterbridge, Juma Santos, Karen Briggs, Karen McDonald, Kathy Allmond, Kenny Elliot, Kevin Ricard, Larry and Luisa Dunn, Leon Mobley, Lil John Roberts, Leslie Drayton, Malcolm Weldon, Maisha Grimes, Mark Stevens, Kevin Chokan, Marva King, Maxine Downs, Melvin Davis, Michael Stanton, Natalie Jackson, Nana Vasconseles, Natalie Bullock "Natlocks," Nick Smith, Pat Taylor, Patrice Rushen, Penny, Crystal, and Shanice Wilson, Phyllis Bailey Brooks, Ralph Sutton, Randy Paiget, "Saba" Bobby Elliston, Shanie Baker, Sheila Bryant, Sible Walton, Stanley Clark, Tabula, Taku, Tiffany Barsotti, Todd Cochran, Tony Haynes, Tony Poingsett, Tony Pringle, Tootie Heath, Wanda McNair, Wayne Vaughn, Makada, Will Kennedy and the Yellowjackets ("Thanx fuh hookin me up. I couldn't have donnit witout chu!"), Zack Harmon, Christopher Troy, Diane Patrick, Amanyea Payne, Agbale, Abiola, Freddy Z., Howie Lindeman, Louie Palomo, Karen Guilleno and Magic Shears, Dr. Rosie Milligan, the ADAWE musical group, and all my "Brothas and Sistas from Dahood." (U know who U are, wherevah U are!) Much Love to All Yall!!

If I have left anyone out, know that I love you too, and there will be more to come!

DEDICATION

THIS IS ALSO DEDICATED TO SOME VERY SPECIAL PEOPLE WHO HAVE WORKED ALL THEIR LIFE TO BRING BEAUTY TO THE WORLD, WHO HAVE LEFT US WITH POSITIVE THOUGHTS AND ENCOURGEMENT TO BRING THE BEST OUT OF OURSELVES, AND OTHERS!

EUGENIA "GENIE" JACKSON *My mother and the sweetest person I have ever known in this life, or any other!*

GEORGE HOWARD *Great musician, great friend!*

MILES DAVIS *Great musician, great inspiration, who I've had the pleasure, and blessing of learning from, and working with!*

Yungus and Wolf, Kikinit.

Biography

Darryl Munyungo Jackson, is professional musician. He makes his living creating sounds on instruments that you beat, strike, shake, blow, pluck, and stroke!

A native of Los Angeles, California, Munyungo has traveled throughout the world sharing his expertise with many people. For over 30 years he has recorded, performed, and traveled with artist such as The Supremes, Temptations, Four Tops, Patti LaBelle, Aretha Franklin, The Pointer Sisters, Anita Baker, Kenny Loggins, Sting, Miles Davis, Stevie Wonder, Lionel Richie, Jonathan Butler, George Howard and Dianne Reeves, just to name a few.
Munyungo releases his first book, "The Nu Naybahood Funetic Ebonic Dictionary."

Darryl "Wolf" Jackson Jr., besides being an excellent cartooonist, is also a "mix master," rapper and composer. In his short career, he has worked on many projects, in many different capacities, including co-production on the "Funky Gripster" track on Ice Tea's "Home Invasion" CD. He also composed the rap for the Bill Cosby "Grape Jell-O" commerical. This is his first project as a cartoonist/illustrator.

B GOOD 2 YOURSELF AND 1 ANUTHA!

BOOK AVAILABLE THROUGH
Milligan Books
An Imprint Of Professional Business
Consulting Service

The Nu Naybahood Funetic
Ebonic Dictionary $13.95

Order Form

Milligan Books
1425 West Manchester, Suite B,
Los Angeles, California 90047
(323) 750-3592

Mail Check or Money Order to:
Milligan Books

Name _____ Date _____

Address _____

City_____ State _____ Zip Code_____

Day telephone _____

Evening telephone_____

Book title _____

Number of books ordered ___ Total cost .... $_____

Sales Taxes (CA Add 8.25%) .... $_____

Shipping & Handling $3.00 per book .... $_____

Total Amount Due..$_____

· Check   · Money Order   Other Cards _____

· Visa   · Master Card   Expiration Date _____

Credit Card No. _____

Driver's License No. _____

Signature _____ Date _____